AS THE TWIG IS BENT

AS
THE TWIG
IS
BENT

Therapeutic Values in the Use of
Drama and the Dramatic in the Church

by

LOUIS DUANE HATFIELD, A.B., M.A.

VANTAGE PRESS   NEW YORK   WASHINGTON   HOLLYWOOD

FIRST EDITION

To my wife, Fran,
Whose love made it a reality

PREFACE

This book is an effort to encourage better appreciation of the therapeutic values inherent in drama and the dramatic in the church. For instance, there is drama in ideas alone. Perry Miller, in the foreword of his volume on the life of Jonathan Edwards, states:

> The real life of Jonathan Edwards was the life of his mind. Hence, in order that the emphasis may fall in the proper measure, this book is focused upon the drama of his ideas, and the external biography is restricted to the basic essentials.[1]

God works through human beings as he does through his other creations. Man is not an end in himself. Man should be free to think and do as long as his liberty does not impinge upon or cause a loss of liberty to others. Hence, he must be a responsible being. With liberty comes responsibility and with responsibility comes the necessity of knowing what we really are. Therefore we should study the therapeutics of drama in the church if we are to encourage and help people to become themselves. This becoming is the challenge of the Sermon on the Mount, or Plain, if you wish.

To begin with, we will lay a foundation of what is good drama and how all drama is religious in that it concerns human beings and their problems. To re-enact experiences is the purpose of drama and whether you are the actor or in the audience you are experiencing life. Hence, a good keyword for this book might be experiential. Dewey calls this pragmatism.

The first part of this book deals with the great dramatist, Shakespeare, whose supreme gift as a dramatist was characterization. If we are to be experiential we should deal with this. In the first chapter we will see that good drama reflects religion. The second chapter discusses a particular aspect of life, guilt and retribution. Then with a summary of the backgrounds of present-day religious drama we close the first part which deals with what good drama is. This part has been limited to one playwright because our book is limited in regard to space.

The second part deals with the therapeutics of drama and the dramatic in the church. Here are chapters on worship as manifested in preaching, the sacraments, prayer, music (hymns, etc.), counseling, and religious drama, followed by a conclusion.

To those wary of the relation of drama, the dramatic, and the mind to the therapeutics afforded by the church let me quote from Jonathan Edwards:

> When the mind is affected with a thing much, it is led into such schemes of thought about it, as, if they were written down, would seem very impertinent to one that was not affected. It is so in all matters. The scripture falls in with the natural stream of one's thought when the mind is affected with the things of which they speak; but are very wide of their series of thought, who are not affected. For instance, the text that says, "one generation passeth away and another cometh, but the earth abideth forever," seems to me in a common frame of mind insipid; the latter part of the verse seems impertinently to be brought in, as what may better tend to illustrate the former; the thought of the earth being the same, does not seem very naturally and affectingly to fall in after the thought of one generation passing, and another coming. What

8

is it to the purpose whether the earth remains the same or no? This makes not the changes of the inhabitants either more or less affecting.

But yet when, upon an occasion, I was more than ordinarily affected with the passing of one generation after another; how all those, who made such a noise and bluster now, and were so much concerned about their life, would be clean gone off from the face of the earth in sixty or seventy years time, and that the world would be left desolate with respect to them, and that another generation would come on, that would be very little concerned about them, and so one after another: it was particularly affecting to me to think that the earth still remained the same through all these changes upon the surface: the same spots of ground, the same mountains and valleys where those things were done, remaining just as they were, though the actors ceased, and the actors just gone. And then this text came into my mind.[2]

Louis Duane Hatfield

Notes *

1. Perry Miller, *Jonathan Edwards*, (New York: William Sloane Associates, Inc., 1949), xi.
2. Ibid., p. 2.

* With the exception of quotations reprinted from works in the public domain all excerpts are used by special permission of the present copyright holders.

CONTENTS

11

ment of Baptism; The Sacrament of Communion,
Prayer: How is prayer to be distinguished, if at
all, from Autosuggestion?; How is Prayer to be
distinguished, if at all, from Interhuman Communication?; What is the Relationship of Prayer to:
Belief; Faith; Action?—Music: Introduction; In-
fluences; Effectiveness; Usage

PART I

WHAT IS GOOD DRAMA?

Chapter 1

GOOD DRAMA REFLECTS RELIGION, AS SEEN IN THE WRITINGS OF SHAKESPEARE

Introduction

Use of Therapy in Shakespeare

"Understanding of Human Behavior Held Essential for Actors and Authors" is the subject of an article entitled "Basic Equipment" by Joseph Kramm. He makes the following observations:

> It is just as correct to refer to Shakespeare as a great psychologist as it is to call him a great playwright. So with Shaw and Ibsen and O'Neill, and those masters of psychology, Molière and Aristophanes.
>
> The science of analysis as evolved by Freud was based on monumental research, intense observation, original thinking and a study of literature. As a matter of fact, there is scarcely any modern work on analysis, whatever the splinter school, that does not quote freely "from the poet" as authority for a particular psychological observation. It seems almost as if the author was saying—"You see, here's the proof—Shakespeare said the same thing—in another way, of course." [1]

What is being said is, there is a use of therapy in the writings of Shakespeare. Yes, a religious therapy if you will. Kramm above points up our argument in the statement that

15

Shakespeare was a great psychologist as well as a great playwright.

He is not alone in this, for two hundred years ago (1753) Samuel Johnson stated in regard to Shakespeare:

> He had looked with great attention to the Scenes of Nature; but his chief Skill was in Human Actions, Passions, and Habits; he was therefore delighted with such Tales as afforded numerous Incidents, and exhibited many Characters, in many Changes of Situation. These Characters are so copiously diversified, and some of them so justly pursued, that his Works may be considered as a Map of Life, a faithful Miniature of human Transactions, and he that has read Shakespear with Attention, will perhaps find little new in the crowded World.
>
> Among his other Excellencies it ought to be remarked, because it has hitherto been unnoticed, that his Heroes are Men, that the Love and Hatred, the Hopes and Fears of his chief Personages are such as are common to other Human Beings, and not like those which later Times have exhibited, peculiar to Phantoms that strut upon the Stage.
>
> It is not perhaps very necessary to enquire whether the Vehicle of so much Delight and Instruction be a Story probable, or unlikely, native, or foreign. Shakespear's Excellence is not the Fiction of a Tale, but the Representation of Life; and his Reputation is therefore safe, till Human Nature shall be changed.[2]

This last quotation, used by Stewart in his introduction to *Character and Motive in Shakespeare*, bears out his suggestion that "Shakespeare understood the passions and described, or conveyed, their several and conjoined operations with certainty, subtlety and power."[3]

Strong, in *The Great Poets and Their Theology*, feels that "After earnest searching I can unhesitatingly avow the belief that the great dramatist was both pure in his moral teaching and singularly sound in faith." [4]

Further:

> As to imagery, I run no risk in saying that our poet saw nothing in an isolated way. To him there was a universe: all things were interdependent; truth in one realm had its analogues in every other. It was not the mere association of ideas which we call fancy; it was the discernment of rational connections which we call imagination. [5]
>
> Our Lord Jesus Christ was the most imaginative, and at the same time the most profound, of thinkers: bread, water, light, darkness, the sea, the sky, the birds, the beasts, the fish of the sea, all taught spiritual lessons. Shakespeare possessed this divine gift of imagination in his lower degree and within his more limited range. The flow of metaphor is so constant and so natural that we cannot call it brilliancy—it is insight into the heart of things. [6]

This sounds much to me like Carl R. Rogers' empathy. For without imagination the entering into another's experience is an impossibility. Rogers in the preface to his volume *Client-Centered Therapy* says: "Therapy is of the essence of life, and is to be so understood." [7]

Everyone does not have the opportunity to view the plays of Shakespeare on the stage and screen; therefore they should be considered in the reading, to see if they do register a feeling of therapy. In an article on "Devotional Literature" Russell L. Dicks speaks in evaluating devotional material:

> A third principle is that devotional literature must come to grips with life situations and living. I suppose this is what we mean when we say an idea is sound psychologically, although I am not quite sure what that means, for psychology, like philosophy, has many

facets, and what is sound for one may not be for another. Coming to grips with life means being realistic without being sordid.[8]

Below, I quote Moulton in his *Introduction to the Literature of the Bible:*

> To take simple illustrations. A reader is using a chapter of the Bible as a devotional exercise, striving to bring home to his heart what he reads as a Divine message. He has omitted to note that the portion of *Job* from which he has selected his chapter opened with the words, "Then answered Bildad the Shuhite:" and, in the final chapter of the book, God is represented as declaring that this Bildad and the other friends of Job "have not spoken of him the thing that is right." Thus this devotional exercise is seeking to realize as God's message the words of a speaker whom God himself expressly repudiates. The mistake has arisen simply from overlooking the dramatic form of the book; in other literature the details represent the author's sentiments, in drama they represent the sentiments which the author has put into the mouth of another, possibly of one who is the opposite of himself. The author of *Job* is no more responsible for the sentiments of Bildad than Shakespeare is to be credited with the horrible thoughts of Iago.[9]

An individual's personal experience is extremely limited. He is a product of his conditioning: his physical constitution, the health of his parents, the degree of their compatibility, the extent to which they accept and understand him, their economic and social status, the mores of the neighbors—in short, biological, psychological, and sociological factors have all contributed to the shaping of his personality. But these need not be limiting forces. The subtle process of identification which drama affords will permit him sympathetically to enter the lives of others and become immeasurably enriched through his analysis of their motives and drives, hopes, and fears, loves and hates. He will thus come better to understand the elements of his own personality and the conflicting forces that impel men as individuals and as members of society.

Implicit in drama are all of the facts of psychology. The facts constitute the center of the experience which is literature. But the facts alone are not truth. They become true to the scientist as his imagination plays upon them and weaves them together into a consistent and organic whole. They become true to the poet or the dramatist when his imagination has ordered them into a living organism. But the layman cannot readily enter into the imagination of the scientist, for the scientist separates the parts of human knowledge, and only those who share his technical equipment can see the whole. All persons are privileged, however, to enter into the imaginative experience of the artist, for art relates all knowledge to human experience. Art, like poetry, attaches emotion to the idea; the idea is the fact! All those who possess the capacity of the artist, not as creator or draftsman, but as human being, can share his understanding. The artist writing as a man to men calls into exercise our universal heritage of love and hatred, hope and fear. He alone can communicate to the emotions as well as to the intellect our common experience of life. While the scientist draws upon the fact and the case study, thus treating of the partial and the exceptional, the artist, dealing with the same material by an imaginative process of selection and synthesis, presents a higher fact—that truth which is universal and functional.

We shall therefore let the artist, Shakespeare, be our guide. At one time he may use the methods of the empiricist, recording human behavior in action; at another time he may employ introspection, setting down the thoughts of human beings. But always he is the creator whose power it is to impress the reader or his audience with the universality of basic human experience.

19

Since the abnormal and exceptional in human behavior have contributed to our understanding of the normal and representative, we will not confine our attention to the latter. It is true that the majority of people do not undergo the emtional conflicts of a character in a Shakespearean drama, but it does not thereby follow that a Richard III or an Othello is untrue to life. In experiencing their extreme torment, before which our own love and hatred, hope and fear, may dwindle to insignificance, we come better to understand our own emotions. The Aristotelian theory of catharsis propounded over two thousand years ago, no less than the concepts of Freud, suggests that sharing another's experience may purge us of our own hatred and fear and permit us to release in pity some of our aggressive drives. If we understand why people are impelled to brutality or self-torture or antisocial behavior, we can less easily revel in our own superiority and self-righteously condemn the victims of such impulses. Only when we learn to assign adequate causes to man's behavior and perceive the significance of his acts in the context of his total personality, shall we ourselves be substituting for irrational emotional reactions the cognitive, investigative powers of our higher faculties.

We recognize in Shakespearean drama patterns of emotions common to us today. The artist has imposed design on the raw materials of life, and in his detached view we may find insight into the problems of our own lives. Through the vicarious experiences of Shakespearean drama, we may approach that inward and outward integration of self which it is the purpose of therapy to foster. We may see that neither the individual nor environment is static and unalterable, but subject to change and interaction, and that man may have some power to direct himself and his world.

The continuity of our quotations, the observations regarding them and the summation above, it is hoped, will encourage the reader to the conclusion suggested: that there is a use of therapy in the dramas of Shakespeare. We will now attempt to deal briefly with four religious concepts as they are reflected in the writings of Shakespeare. They are: Love and

Hatred, Hope and Fear. Since these overlap in their relations we will not be able to separate them topically so instead we shall deal with them as they appear in three of Shakespeare's plays, namely: *King Henry the Sixth, King Richard the Third,* and *Othello.*

Love and Hatred, Hope and Fear as Portrayed in the Character of Richard, Duke of Gloucester, afterwards Richard III

Physical Heritage

Dowden paints Richard's character:

> There is something sublime and terrible in so great and fierce a human energy as that of Richard, concentrated within one withered and distorted body. This is the evil offspring and flower of the long and cruel wars—this distorted creature, a hater and scorner of man, an absolute cynic, loveless and alone, disregarding all human bonds and human affections, yet full of intellect, of fire, of power.[10]

Certain physical characteristics—personal appearance, the state of his health, a physical deformity—may influence an individual's personality and determine the nature of his attitudes toward himself and others. The color of his hair, the shape of his nose, the size of his bones—innumerable physical details—may be important as they serve to attract or repel people. Physical defects often assume undue significance because of a sensitiveness induced in childhood by the attitude of parents, companions, or teachers.

Chambers tells us:

> Richard is, indeed, a consummate actor. The whole secret of his success lies in the adroitness with which he plays upon the ambitions and weaknesses of those whom he intends to make his puppets, in the audacity

21

with which he flings himself into the appropriate utterances of sentiments the most foreign to his nature. And
how he revels in it, in his command of himself, in his
betraying silences and ironical speech, in the fine sense
of dramatic values with which he chooses the moment
to strike his blows.[11]

Fears, repression, introversion, despondency, self-pity,
emotional outbursts, efforts at compensation, and daydream-
ing may become more serious obstacles to satisfactory adjustment to the world than are the physical defects themselves.
Moulton feels about Richard that

His choice is only between different modes of
villainy, never between villainy and honesty.[12]

Whether one accepts a physical handicap and adjusts himself to it or allows it to warp his mind and emotions, its
presence must leave a deep mark on the individual's personality.

The compensatory mechanisms which one may build into
his character to make up for physical handicaps were well
understood by Shakespeare, who has given us remarkable insight into the problem in the character of Richard III. In two
passages, first in *Henry the Sixth*, the third part, Act V,
Scene vi, Line 34 through Line 93 and again in *Richard the
Third*, Act I, Scene i, Line 1 through Line 41, he has traced
Richard's resolution to be a villain to his realization that his
physical deformity will never permit him to play the coveted
role of lover, that he is perforce a social outcast and can
assert his personality only through attaining ruthless power
over the lives of others.

Gervinus states:

Had he been endowed with the same favor of
nature as his father, Richard would have developed the

22

same good qualities which the father possessed in addition to his dangerous gifts.[13]

Summary

What happened to the person? He, Richard, born crippled and deformed, was the object of severe scorn in the eyes of others as well as his own.

What did it do to him? It caused him to become a murderer and to make wickedness and violence his pastime.

What could have been done for him? In his case those who cared for and instructed him as a child should not have indulged in superstitious chatter. This mistake clearly appears in his remarks in later life.

Parallel in Literature. Quasimodo, the Hunchback of Notre Dame, character in *Notre Dame de Paris* by Victor Hugo speaks, "Oh! All that I have ever loved!" [14] Quasimodo makes this statement after thrusting the archdeacon over the tower of the great church and as he looks into the distance at the figure of Esmeralda hanging on the gallows.

*Love and Hatred, Hope and Fear as Portrayed in the
Character of Othello, the Moor of Venice*

Emotional Conflicts

1600 to 1605 must be regarded as the most productive half-decade in the history of literature. For during this half-decade were produced *Antony and Cleopatra, Hamlet, Lear, Macbeth, Othello,* and *Coriolanus.* Here are the six greatest tragedies of the world. They represent the excessive working of the greatest passions. In *Antony and Cleopatra* we see sensual pleasure dragging down a noble mind and heart; in *Macbeth* it is ambition; in *Othello* jealousy; in *Coriolanus* pride. *Lear* shows the human spirit driven to insanity by filial ingratitude;

23

Hamlet is the impersonation of idealistic wavering in the presence of duty, and of opportunity forever lost.[15]

Bradley asks:

What is the peculiarity of *Othello?* What is the distinctive impression that it leaves? Of all Shakespeare's tragedies, I would answer, not even excepting *King Lear, Othello* is the most painfully exciting and the most terrible. From the moment when the temptation of the hero begins, the reader's heart and mind are held in a vise, experiencing the extremes of pity and fear, sympathy and repulsion, sickening hope and dreadful expectation.[16]

Further Bradley states:

But *Othello* is a drama of modern life; when it first appeared it was a drama almost of contemporary life, for the date of the Turkish attack on Cyprus is 1570. The characters come close to us, and the application of the drama to ourselves (if the phrase may be pardoned) is more immediate than it can be in *Hamlet* or *Lear*.[17]

Our emotions are the inner forces that move us—the powerful drives of love and hatred, hope and fear, with their infinitely complex variations of jealousy, pity, anxiety, tenderness, and innumerable other feelings that manage to keep us in a stirred-up state much of the time. Convenient though it would be, one cannot fit into sharply differentiated categories anything so complex as human emotions. To say that here is an indiivdual whose reactions are wholly emotional, there another whose responses are totally rational, is to ignore the truth that behavior may be measured only in relation to the functioning of the entire organism. One's emotions cannot be divorced from the whole of one's life. They are inextricably interwoven with drives of self-preservation, sex-expression, and food-getting—in short, with the individual's fundamental human needs. While physical characteristics may exercise considerable influence upon one's emotional reactions, as has already been suggested, one's behavior may be modified by learned adaptations to one's environment. Since the sex drive is given its direction in the early years of the child's life, one important key to emotional behavior lies in the attitudes and interrelationships within the family. And because self-preservation and food-getting are primary drives of every human being, the social and economic structure of society cannot be overlooked in attaching responsibility for man's actions.

Stewart delineates this as Shakespeare's forte:

> Shakespeare's characters—this character and that character—often have far more "psychology" than historical realism would suppose. And, in so far as this holds, Shakespeare's drama is naturalistic in a simple, if not in the simplest, signification: it gives individuals as a profoundly intuitive mind is aware of them. But perhaps none of Shakespeare's great plays is merely naturalistic in this sense; and he does freely use characters like Iago who have at times, and as independent beings, no more psychology than Stoll is prepared to allow them. Nevertheless these characters are composed into a whole which, I think, has psychology, or which is in the total impression an image of life. Iago is unreal, and Stoll is right about him. Othello is unreal, and Stoll is right about him also. But the two together and in interaction are not unreal. The two together make your mind, or mine.[18]

While psychologists generally agree that love and hatred, hope and fear, are the primary emotions, so conditioned are these drives by other aspects of the personality that one never

25

finds them manifested in what might be called a pure or unadulterated state. In his earliest years the child discovers that certain of his desires are acceded to, others are denied. Early expressions of rage—the anger or hatred of the infant whose physical needs or desires meet some obstacle, the aggressive impulses revealed by the older child in his play—are overt emotional expressions. As he grows, the individual learns to control or divert his emotional energy—perhaps to use biting words instead of blows when his desires are thwarted, when his activities in work or play are interfered with, or when some social situation arises which makes him appear ridiculous or inferior. If he finds no acceptable outlet for his feelings of rage and frustration, they may become destructive, turned either in upon himself or outward upon society.

Moulton points us to Shakespeare's Othello—

> To such simplicity of nature human character appears only simple; men must be classified as sheep or goats; there is good and evil only, without fine shadings or neutral colours, without compromises or allowances. Let Desdemona once appear guilty, and all the whiteness of her soul is the white hypocrisy that makes the black all the blacker. So the true love of Othello and Desdemona ends in murder and suicide: though even these are scarcely more terrible than for a love to end in jealousy.[19]

—while Bradley suggests:

> An ineradicable instinct of justice, rather than any last quiver of hope, leads him to question Emilia; but nothing could convince him now, and there follows the dreadful scene of accusation; and then, to allow us the relief of burning hatred and burning tears, the interview of Desdemona with Iago, and that last talk of hers with Emilia, and her last song.[20]

Our fears are probably largely learned, the result of our physical and social conditioning. In a great variety of forms

26

and in varying degrees of intensity, they complicate life for us, driving us to many responses, from the simple reaction of running away to elaborate rationalizations of our conduct. Since most fears are learned, they may also be eliminated through understanding and facing them—a need vital to the development of a healthy personality.

Bradley tells us what directs Othello:

> No doubt the thought of another man's possessing the woman he loves is intolerable to him; no doubt the sense of insult and the impulse of revenge are at times most violent; and these are the feelings of jealousy proper. But these are not the chief or the deepest source of Othello's suffering. It is the wreck of his faith and his love. It is the feeling,
>
> > If she be false, oh then Heaven mocks itself:
>
> the feeling,
>
> > O Iago, the pity of it, Iago!
>
> the feeling,
> But there where I have garner'd up my heart
> Where either I must live, or bear no life;
> The fountain from the which my current runs,
> Or else dries up—to be discarded thence.[21]

The emotions of love and hope continually drive one to seek an object upon which they may be expended. We note how the child's first experience of love in the home may determine his subsequent emotional patterns. Not only his relation to his parents as the first objects of his affection, but his awareness of their relation to each other will indelibly affect his attitudes. He has been a witness, not always a conscious one, to their relationship, sensing their happiness or their misery. As he grows older, he observes the lives of those outside of the family circle more and more. He learns what is regarded as socially acceptable, what is merely expedient, what is criminal. His primary drives thus become subservient to repressive forces. Unconsciously his impulses will be modified to conform with the dictates of his conscience or the mandates of society. Or by the process of sublimation, his emotion may be directed away from its primitive objectives to socially approved goals in friendship, devotion to the arts, achievement in work of social usefulness, love of man, of country, or of God.

Moulton points us to the height of Othello's thought:

> In the middle of the middle act comes the central turning point with the words:
>
>> Excellent wretch! Perdition catch my soul,
>> But I do love thee! and when I love thee not,
>> Chaos is come again.
>
> The tide of Othello's love has reached its height, and from here the ebb begins. And of course it is in the fifth act that we get the outer change, or 'catastrophe,' where the tragic consummation gives place to the reaction upon Iago.[22]

On the other hand, the emotions of love and hope may encounter obstacles which result in repression rather than overt or sublimated expression. They may become entangled with feelings of hatred or fear.

An ambivalent attitude is clearly revealed in Othello. Shakespeare reveals this in Act III, Scene iii, Line 29 through Line 480. Look particularly at the moment Othello protests that he will not be governed by his emotions but rather by his reason: "I'll see before I doubt; when I doubt, prove; and, on the proof, there is no more but this,—away at once with love or jealousy!" [23] Still he is taken in by Iago's diabolical machinations. He cannot separate his love of Desdemona from his hate of her, nor can he summon his intellect to temper his passion. He is making what the psychologist Rivers calls the protopathic response to a stimulus, one in which the separation of the emotional and cognitive aspects of the personality induces an all or nothing response.

Chambers says:

> . . . the fall of Othello is not merely the fall of a good man, but the purposed and inevitable defeat of goodness itself.[24]

Summary

What happened to the person? Othello is taken in by Iago's scheming, who plants carefully the seeds which lead Othello to believe Desdemona untrue to him.

What did it do to him? The seeds of hatred planted by Iago arouse in Othello the play of passions where love and hate fight for the upper hand using jealousy as their tool.

What could have been done for him? Othello should have used reason. He should have investigated the issue, and particularly the motive that Iago had in bearing such unpleasant news to him. The intellect should be so developed that it stands one in good stead at times like these.

An explanation in the field of psychology:

> In all these situations where projection is used, and other people are regarded as bad instead of oneself, it will be clear that the villain of the piece, the rival or whoever it may be who is serving us as a receptacle for our own dangerous and unwanted features, actually becomes to us unconsciously the evil part of ourselves, the "double" of that side of us. This process is often very clear in drama and literature, where such personifications form the stock-in-trade of the writer. Iago, for instance, represents Othello's own greedy impulses, which also are subtly indicated in the unconscious symbolic significance of Othello's blackness.[25]

29

Notes *

1. *New York Times*, July 20, 1952, Sec. 2, p.x. (Joseph Kramm is the author of the 1951-1952 Pulitzer Prize-winning play, *The Shrike*.)

2. J. I. M. Stewart, *Character and Motive in Shakespeare*. (New York: Longmans, Green and Co., 1949), p. 1.

3. *Ibid.*

4. Augustus Hopkins Strong, *The Great Poets and Their Theology*. (Philadelphia: American Baptist Publication Society. 1897), p. 210.

5. *Ibid.*

6. *Ibid.*

7. Carl R. Rogers, *Client-Centered Therapy*. (Boston: Houghton Mifflin Company, 1951), p. x.

8. Russell L. Dicks, "Devotional Literature in Pastoral Care," *Pastoral Psychology*, February 1950, p. 47.

9. Richard G. Moulton, *A Short Introduction to the Literature of the Bible*. (Boston: D. C. Heath and Company, Publishers, 1909), pp. 6 and 7.

10. E. Dowden, *Shakespere in the Literature Primers*. (New York: American Book Company, n.d.), p. 79.

11. E. K. Chambers, *Shakespeare: A Survey*. (London: Sedgwick & Jackson, Ltd., 1925), pp. 16 and 17. Copyright: The Macmillan Company, New York.

12. R. G. Moulton, *Shakespeare as a Dramatic Artist*. (Oxford: At The Clarendon Press, 1906), p. 91.

13. G. G. Gervinus, *Shakespeare Commentaries*. (London: Smith, Elder and Company, 1892), p. 129.

14. Victor Hugo, *Notre Dame de Paris*. (New York and Boston: H. M. Caldwell and Company, n.d.), p. 305.

15. Strong, *op. cit.*, p. 181.

* With the exception of quotations reprinted from works in the public domain all excerpts are used by special permission of the present copyright holders.

16. A. C. Bradley, *Shakespearean Tragedy*. (London: Macmillan & Co., Ltd. 1904), p. 176. Copyright: St. Martin's Press, New York.

17. *Ibid.*, p. 180.

18. Stewart, *op. cit.*, pp. 109 and 110.

19. Moulton, *op. cit.*, p. 230.

20. Bradley, *op. cit.*, p. 197.

21. *Ibid.*, p. 194.

22. Moulton, *op. cit.*, p. 240.

23. George Lyman Kittredge (ed.), *The Complete Works of Shakespeare*, (Boston: Ginn & Co., 1936), *Othello*, Act III, Scene iii, Lines 190-191-192.

24. Chambers, *op. cit.*, p. 220.

25. M. Klein and J. Rivière. *Love, Hate and Reparation.* (London: Hogarth Press, Ltd., 1937), p. 37.

Chapter 2

GOOD DRAMA SUCH AS SHAKESPEARE'S DEALS
CREATIVELY AND EFFECTIVELY WITH SUCH
REDEMPTIVE DOCTRINES AS GUILT
AND RETRIBUTION

Introduction

Shakespeare is credited with being a great student of
human life, and he was, indeed, but not a systematic one.
Perhaps he did formulate logical criticisms of man and his
protean character, but if so it was with Burbage and Ben at
the Boar's Head and not in his plays. Like Plato, he was an
artist first of all. And in his plays, we see him depicting the
wiles men use to get the better of others (and of themselves);
but we see what Shakespeare the man thought about these
characters only when we peer behind the scenes, what scenes
there were, of the "wooden O."

We search for his notions about retribution in the plays,
and it's somewhat of a quest for a will-o'-the-wisp. Bald
indeed when presented on the stage are the concrete evidences of "this even-handed justice" [1] which bends wicked
devices making them "return to plague the inventor." [2] But
just what did Shakespeare think? It's hard to say, for even
as we have the tables turned on such men as Iago and Richard
III, we have also Cordelia slain and Desdemona murdered,
and a sensuous and ribald old malefactor like Falstaff, though
rejected by his one-time boon companion in roistering, shuffl-

ing off peacefully in bed (as Dame Quickly described him) "babbling of green fields." [3]

It's an invitation to philosophize that we get from the thirty-seven plays—if all were his—but there is no sure ground for firm conviction about what Shakespeare himself believed.

In his excellent little book, *Intimations of Immortality in the Sonnets of Shakespeare*, which was delivered as the Ingersoll lecture in 1912, George Herbert Palmer speaks of Shakespeare as a theologian:

> Did he mean to announce a theological doctrine with three stages of successively larger hope? No; he certainly never meant that, but never-the-less it meant him. And just because he had not intended to be a philosophic teacher, but gave his mind wholeheartedly to the lovely boy (i.e., of the sonnets) and his own temptation, I have thought him to be a suitable person to invite to this platform. . . . Few writers of our language, I suppose, are so little theological as he; few so little disposed to report their own beliefs. He is therefore, an unbiased and typical witness to the necessity and meaning of immortality. In the exigencies of the day he has come upon it. Mortality has proved unthinkable. [4]

What Palmer says of Shakespeare's thoughts of immortality is certainly true of his treatment of retribution. "It meant him. . . . In the exigencies of the day he has come upon it." [5] It is unthinkable that we should sow—and not reap. "Whether the story related is fact or fiction makes no difference." [6] It has a likeness to reality; and while Shakespeare's attention was not fixed on retribution, as ours is now, he was busy with the lives wherein this principle is embodied. In the exigencies of the day he has come upon it. And herein we extract the principle "he has come upon." [7]

We must not think, however, that the matter can be settled by what the characters in the drama say. It is ever the mark of the great dramatist that he loses himself in the beings he creates. He does not use them as disguises for himself. Rather it is as though he were listening to them speaking and faithfully recording their words.

Perhaps one can get at the mind of Dante or Milton through the *Inferno* or *Paradise Lost;* but not so can one get at Shakespeare. His characters live, having minds of their own; no puppets they, controlled by strings jerked by an external hand; rather they are free, and their speech wells up from what they are. Hence, to choose isolated sayings of the dramatis personae and find in them the teachings of the drama, is to misconstrue the dramatic genius.

King Lear affords illustration of the matter. Ask the characters of that tempestuous drama if God rules the world. Edmund will answer:

> This is the excellent foppery of this world, that, when we are sick in fortune,—often the surfeits of our own behaviour,—we make guilty of our disasters the sun, the moon, and the stars as if we were guilty on necessity, fools by heavenly compulsion, knaves, thieves, and teachers by spherical predominance, drunkards, liars, and adulterers, by enforc'd obedience of planetary influence, and all that we are evil in by a divine thrusting on. An admirable evasion.[8]

Kent says:

It is the stars,
The stars above us, govern our condition.[9]

Gloucester will put it differently:

As flies to wanton boys are to th' gods.
They kill us for their sport.[10]

Albany says:

This shows you are above,
You justicers, that these our nether crimes
So speedily can venge! [11]

And again he says:

All friends shall taste
The wages of their virtue, and all foes
The cup of their deservings.[12]

Edgar says:

Think that the clearest gods, who make them honours
Of men's responsibilities, have preserv'd thee.[13]

And:

The gods are just, and of our pleasant vices
Make instruments to scourge us.[14]

Add to these lines from *Lear* the familiar words of Hamlet:

There's a divinity that shapes our ends,
Rough-hew them how we will.[15]

The answer, then, to a question like this—did Shakespeare think God ruled the world?—would be a series of contradictions. Hence, one may not combine utterances of dramatic characters to find out Shakespeare's thought.

How then shall we extract Shakespeare's thought about retribution? Perhaps it would be better to state the matter in another form. Let us see wherein his plays lend themselves to the ideas we have about retribution, foregoing any notions about deciding that thus and so did Shakespeare think. Humbly, then, we set about the task, confessing that we

cannot know what the master of those who write would say
was his conclusion about retribution.

Generalities

Two preliminary remarks should be made at this junc-
ture. The *first* of them is that Shakespeare seems to say that
the universe itself is antagonistic towards the evildoer and is
profoundly disturbed by the commission of wickedness on the
earthly plane. "The stars in their courses fought against
Sisera." [16] Portentous signs and omens accompany or precede
the evil deeds of men. Witness the warning of Hubert to
King John:

> My Lord, they say five moons were seen tonight:
> Four fixed, and the fifth did whirl about
> The other four in wondrous motion. . . .

> Old men and beldames in the streets
> Do prophesy upon it dangerously.
> Young Arthur's death is common in their mouths;
> And when they talk of him, they shake their heads
> And whisper one another in the ear;
> And he that speaks doth gripe the hearer's wrist,
> Whilst he that hears makes fearful action
> With wrinkled brows, with nods, with rolling eyes.
> I saw a smith stand with his hammer, thus,
> The whilst his iron did on the anvil cool,
> With open mouth swallowing a tailor's news,
> Who, with his shears and measure in his hand,
> Standing on slippers, which his nimble haste
> Had falsely thrust upon contrary feet,
> Told of a many thousand warlike French
> That were embattailed and rank'd in Kent.
> Another lean unwash'd artificer
> Cuts off his tale and talks of Arthur's death. [17]

36

Calpurnia recounts to Julius Caesar the omens predictive of the death of a mighty prince:

A lioness hath whelped in the streets,
And graves have yawn'd, and yielded up their dead;
Fierce fiery warriors fought upon the clouds,
In ranks and squadrons and right form of war,
Which drizzled blood upon the Capitol;
The noise of battle hurtled in the air,
Horses did neigh, and dying men did groan,
And ghosts did shriek and squeal about the streets,
O Caesar,

When beggars die there are no comets seen;
The heavens themselves blaze forth the death of princes.[18]

And outside Macbeth's castle Ross and an Old Man discuss the deep damnation of King Duncan's taking off:

Ah, good father,
Thou seest the heavens, as troubled with man's act,
Threaten his bloody stage. By th' clock 'tis day,
And yet dark night strangles the traveling lamp

And the Old Man replies:

'Tis unnatural,
Even like the deed that's done. On Tuesday last
A falcon, tow'ring in her pride of place,
Was by a mousing owl hawk'd at and kill'd.

Ross adds his evidence of disturbed nature:

And Duncan's horses (a thing most strange and certain),
Beauteous and swift, the minions of their race,
Turn'd wild in nature, broke their stalls, flung out,
War with mankind.

37

Old Man:

'Tis said they eat each other.

Ross:

They did so, to th' amazement of mine eyes
That look'd upon't.[19]

Perhaps the most famous of all the external disturbances
of nature that correspond to the inward turmoil of man is
in the storm scene of *King Lear*.

"Lear and the Fool appear. Lear is quite mad:" [20] So indicate two editors' stage directions. All the tempestuous forces
of nature are loosed to lash the aged monarch, maddened by
the infidelity of those he had placed his fond trust in. A
tempest-driven soul is roaming mad in a tempest-driven
world. The universe itself is agitated, in the world of Shakespeare, by the commission of wicked deeds.

The *second* remark that needs to be made is this: Shakespeare implies that while the universe itself may be against
the evildoer, man is responsible for his own evil actions.
Evidence the famous statement in *Julius Caesar*, when Cassius
of the "lean and hungry look" [21] speaks to noble Brutus:

Men at some time are masters of their fates.
The fault, dear Brutus, is not in our stars,
But in ourselves, that we are underlings.[22]

Popular thought would still place the responsibility for
man's recalcitrance on something outside himself. The ety-
mology of disaster is *stars against*. But when one delves deep
in Shakespeare, he sees the tragedies that ensue upon the
wicked deeds of men rather, in Karl Menninger's words, as
Man Against Himself.[23] Man is responsible for his own evil

actions, and the retribution that follows hard upon deeds grows out of what man is.

It may seem as though this conclusion were belied by the presence in the plays of supernatural visitants, of apparitions that bespeak an unearthly control over the affairs of men. There is the ghost of Hamlet's father, for example, the shades of Richard III's victims and the weird witches of Macbeth, along with the spectre of the murdered Banquo. Indeed, these spirits do hint that life is more mysterious than we know, but they are really used as outward symbols of an inward state. Perhaps Shakespeare thought of them as objective, yet he did not use them to control the actions of his characters but to reveal their thoughts, or exercise a suggestive power. But this unseen power is not fate. To one reader, at least, the great tragedies do not speak of predetermination.

But accident will play its part. Tremendous consequences are made to follow from the sheerest chance. A chance encounter with a pirate ship brought Hamlet back to Denmark; Juliet awoke from her unconsciousness a moment too late; the friar's message to Romeo accidentally miscarried; had Edgar arrived a moment sooner the life of Cordelia would have been saved; if Duncan had not stayed the night in Macbeth's castle, he would have lived on; Desdemona dropped her handkerchief and tragic events ensued; so, on and on, the list of accidents grows throughout the plays. It is what is called tychism, the element of chance in human life.

We can pass over the lesser plays with a few remarks. Suffice it to say that, in the exigencies of the day, Shakespeare came upon retribution in these. *Titus Andronicus* is one of the earliest of them, a lurid melodrama wherein the—literally—black villain, Aaron, spins a web of violence around Titus and his family. It is a drama of amputated hands and tongues torn out, of lust, rapine, murder, horror. But even here, amid the extravagance of speech and violent action,

See justice done on Aaron, that damn'd Moor,
By whom our heavy haps had their beginning.[24]

39

Even here we find Shakespeare with the thought of Hosea in his mind, "For they have sown the wind, and they shall reap the whirlwind:" [25]

Likewise in one of the three unfeeling farces, as Mark Van Doren [26] calls them, in *The Merry Wives of Windsor*, we see fat Falstaff who has tried to be his bawdy worst suffering the indignity of being carried out with dirty linen in a buck basket by the merry wives of the village.

Specifics

However fruitful an examination of the rest of the lesser dramas would be, as, for example, the magnificent chronicles, we must concentrate on those more familiar to all of us.

Of the so-called joyous comedies, consider only *Much Ado About Nothing*. A clue to the nature of the play may be found in the title. In Elizabethan days nothing was pronounced like our contemporary *noting*. It was a play on words, for noting meant eavesdropping, and here indeed is much ado about eavesdropping, or the eavesdroppers eavesdropped. The perpetrator of the near-tragedy is repaid in his own coin. The villainous Don John blackens, by his machinations, the character of Hero, making her to appear to give midnight boudoir hospitality to strange men when, seemingly virtuous, she is affianced to a gentleman, Claudio.

Chance plays its part, and the comedy would have been a tragedy had Borachio been less expansive or even if he had chosen a better place for his confidences. The stupid but loveable Dogberry and the insufferable yokels who compose the town watch overhear Borachio reveal the plot to blacken Hero's character. All the plot thus far has been worked out by a series of events wherein one person eavesdrops on another. Now the stupid watch eavesdrops on the cunning conspirators and foils them. Their methods may be crude and overladen with painfully tedious malapropisms; they plumb the depths of nightmare wit; but their inept blundering saves Hero's character and restores her in the eyes of her father and Claudio. What cunning envy ties, stupidity unties. "But God hath chosen the foolish things of the world to confound the wise; and God hath chosen the weak things of the world to confound the things which are mighty." [27]

Here is the converse of the situation, pointed out from Homer's *Iliad*,[28] wherein the goddess Pallas Athena deceives Hector to his doom at the hands of Achilles. It was the gods intervening in the affairs of men regardless of their merits, and wreaking havoc. But in *Much Ado*, we have chance playing its part, and that chance working for good.

The Merchant of Venice is familiar to us principally for its famous character, Shylock, the Jew, who tried to get his pound of flesh. Although modern actors have interpreted him as a pitiable figure eliciting our sympathies, he was no doubt meant in those days to be somewhat ridiculous. Nevertheless, to the modern reader or playgoer, he cannot remain so; he is rather the immemorial Jew, hard-bestead and faulty, calling forth mingled compassion and censure.

Part of the motive of Shylock in seeking vengeance upon the merchant lies in the detection of his daughter and her elopement with Lorenzo, a friend of the merchant, bearing some of the Jew's treasures. Thus it is described in one scene:

I never heard a passion so confus'd,
So strange, outrageous, and so variable,
As the dog Jew did utter in the streets.
'My daughter! O my ducats! O my daughter!
Fled with a Christian! O my Christian ducats!
Justice! the law! My ducats, and my daughter!
A sealed bag, two sealed bags of ducats,
Of double ducats, stol'n from me by my daughter!

Justice! Find the girl!' [29]

The scene is reminiscent of an incident recounted in Genesis. Jacob, wealthy now through his dealings with his father-in-law, takes his departure with his wives, Leah and

41

Rachel, during the absence of Laban. Rachel purloins her father's idol, and in consternation Laban comes hurrying after to Mizpah, where he remonstrates with Jacob, and "Jacob was wroth and chode with Laban." [30] The parallel is brought home by Shylock who earlier recounted the sharp dealings of Jacob and Laban. [31]

Shakespeare could not portray so rich a character as Shylock without endowing him with human qualities. This is what he says:

Signior Antonio, many a time and oft
In the Rialto you have rated me
About my moneys and my usances.
Still have I borne it with a patient shrug;
For suff'rance is the badge of all our tribe.
You call me misbeliever, cutthroat dog,
And spet upon my Jewish gaberdine,
And all for use of that which is mine own.
Well then, it now appears you need my help.
Go to then, you come to me and you say,
'Shylock, we would have moneys': You say so—
You that did void your rheum upon my beard
And foot me as you spurn a stranger cur
Over your threshold. Moneys is your suit.
What should I say to you? Should I not say
'Hath a dog money? Is it possible
A cur can lend three thousand ducats?' or
Shall I bend low, and in a bondman's key,
With bated breath and whisp'ring humbleness,
Say this:
'Fair sir, you spit on me on Wednesday last;
You spurn'd me such a day; another time
You call'd me dog; and for these courtesies
I'll lend you thus much moneys'? [32]

In the third act, when asked why he would extort the bond of a pound of flesh, his pent-up feelings of indignation against his mistreatment wells forth:

To bait fish withal. If it will feed nothing else, it will feed my revenge. He hath disgrac'd me, and hind'red me half a million; laugh'd at my losses, mock'd at my gains, scorned my nation, thwarted my bargains, cooled my friends, heated mine enemies— and what's his reason? I am a Jew. Hath not a Jew eyes? Hath not a Jew hands, organs, dimensions, senses, affections, passions? fed with the same food, hurt with the same weapons, subject to the same diseases, healed by the same means, warmed and cooled by the same winter and summer as a Christian is? If you prick us, do we not bleed? If you tickle us, do we not laugh? If you poison us, do we not die? And if you wrong us, shall we not revenge? If we are like you in the rest, we will resemble you in that. If a Jew wrong a Christian, what is his humility? Revenge. If a Christian wrong a Jew, what should his sufferance be by Christian example? Why, revenge. The villainy you teach me I will execute, and it shall go hard but I will better the instruction.[33]

However justified Shylock may in a manner be in his desire for revenge, he is cunning, vengeful, cruel. Wronged as he may be by the Venetian merchants, he seeks to correct that evil by another wrong. Cunningly he weaves his vindictive web around helpless Antonio, whetting his knife in gleeful anticipation of carving his victim's flesh. He is acting on the old Hebrew *lex talionis.*[34]

Portia, disguised as a judge, eloquently pleads with him to go beyond justice to mercy. Here are contracted two principles which Jesus mentioned in the Sermon on the Mount: the saying of them of old time, "An eye for an eye and a tooth for a tooth:" [35] and the principle of forgiveness, "but whosoever shall smite thee on thy right cheek, turn to him the other also." [36] Shylock was trying to exercise himself what rightfully may be said to belong to God: "To me belongeth vengeance, and recompense:" [37] Thus the speech of Portia hardly needs quotation:

The quality of mercy is not strain'd;
It droppeth as the gentle rain from heaven
Upon the place beneath. It is twice blest—
It blesseth him that gives, and him that takes.
'Tis mightiest in the mightiest. It becomes
The throned monarch better than his crown.
His sceptre shows the force of temporal power,
The attribute to awe and majesty,
Wherein doth sit the dread and fear of kings;

It is an attribute to God himself;
And earthly power doth then show likest God's
When mercy seasons justice. Therefore, Jew,
Though justice be thy plea, consider this—
That, in the course of justice, none of us
Should see salvation. We do pray for mercy,
And that same prayer doth teach us all to render
The deeds of mercy.[38]

Thus Shylock has his chance, fails to grasp it, and inexorable justice is meted out to him. But no one can fail to feel some sympathy for him as he leaves the court-room, the harsh verdict pronounced—a broken old man, complaining, "I am not well." [39]

However sympathetic we moderns may be with Shylock for the wrongs he suffered at Christian hands, we must admit his wrong in seeking vengeance. He sought to undo his enemies, and was caught in the toils of his devices. "Whoso diggeth a pit shall fall therein: and he that rolleth a stone, it will return upon him."[40]

When *Romeo and Juliet* is mentioned, we usually think of the balcony scene with its lovely poetry, or the tragedy of these two "star-crossed lovers" [41] whom chance betrayed. But it is more than that. It may be read as a drama with an environing action of hate and revenge that embroiled two famous houses of Verona, and how that hate created more bitter vengeance, more harsh hatred, until one member of each house broke the vicious circle with their love. As the prologue puts it:

> Two households, both alike in dignity,
>   In fair Verona, where we lay our scene,
> From ancient grudge break to new mutiny,
>   Where civil blood makes civil hands unclean.
> From forth the fatal loins of these two foes
>   A pair of star-cross'd lovers take their life;
> Whose misadventur'd piteous overthrows
>   Doth with their death bury their parents' strife.

> Which, but their children's end, naught could remove.[42]

The Capulets and Montagues have striven together until their ill-feeling has moved the Prince of Verona to threaten them:

> Three civil brawls, bred of an airy word
> By thee, old Capulet, and Montague,
> Have thrice disturb'd the quiet of our streets
> And made Verona's ancient citizens
> Cast by their grave beseeming ornaments
> To wield old partisans, in hands as old,
> Cank'red with peace, to part your cank'red hate.
> If ever you disturb our streets again,
> Your lives shall pay the forfeit of the peace.[43]

It takes no long thinking to see the larger meaning of such a situation as this. Contending houses—or nations—will destroy themselves by their continued strife; the high gift of peace cannot come through mutual hate; only further discord can arise from bitter enmity.

Then Romeo of the house of Montague falls in love with Juliet of the house of Capulet. It is a hopeless love, and one that Juliet thinks "too unadvis'd, too sudden;" [44] but nonetheless it is a powerful love. Through the transforming power of this deep emotion, Juliet changes from a dependent girl to a strong and independent young woman; and Romeo is metamorphosed from a lovesick boy mooning about his Rosaline into a man of strength and dignity. It is always interesting in Shakespeare to see how love enobles his characters—save, perhaps, Troilus and Cressida! He seems to see it as an emotion of immeasurable power. It is so, at least with Romeo and Juliet. "Love never faileth." [45]

I need not trace the plot through all its stages; the main outlines of it are familiar enough to all of us. Suffice it to say that chance plays against these two lovers along with the terrible antagonism of the houses they come from, until at last they both lay dead in the Capulet tomb. The Prince enters and points up the moral of the events. Here has violence returned upon the violent and killed the best of each. So he says:

Where be these enemies? Capulet, Montague,
See what a scourge is laid upon your hate,
That Heaven finds means to kill your joys with love!

All are punish'd.[46]

The recurring cycle of hate creating violence and hate is broken by love. Jesus asked, "How can Satan cast out Satan?" [47] Shakespeare would seem to say the selfsame thing: violence cannot drive out violence. But it is love that heals old wounds and rights distorted relationships. "I say unto you, Love your enemies." [48] This love has wrought its healing power in Romeo and Juliet, and the play ends with the reconciliation of the two houses. Says Capulet: "O brother Montague, give me thy hand." [49]

We would all agree that *Hamlet* is Shakespeare's best-known play. It is a tragedy of revenge, a type of play to which the early *Titus Andronicus* belonged, as well as a long list of contemporary Elizabethan dramas. Shakespeare utilized this melodramatic genre and by his quickening touch great-

46

ened it. Under his hand it became the most famous of his creations, the enigmatic Prince of Denmark strangely appealing to the enthralled imagination of multitudes.

An ambitious man, uncle to the young Hamlet, succeeded in grasping the Danish sceptre by murdering his king-brother. His marriage to the late king's widow followed hard upon the funeral rites.

Here is an unnatural event that at once starts its series of consequences, not merely in political events but more profoundly in the mind of Hamlet. The first repercussions of the act are felt by the young prince. Not yet aware of the real cause of his father's death, but desponding over his mother's overhasty remarriage, he stands melancholy over the weariness of an unprofitable world, like Ecclesiastes with his "all is vanity." [50] It is as though Shakespeare were saying that an evil deed, though not yet known as such, brings its strain and twist into the relationships of men. Hamlet is curtly sarcastic with the king and queen, and when he is alone he gives vent to his dejection:

> O that this too too solid flesh would melt,
> Thaw, and resolve itself into a dew!
> Or that the Everlasting had not fix'd
> His canon 'gainst self-slaughter! O God! God!
> How weary, stale, flat, and unprofitable
> Seem to me all the uses of this world!
> Fie on 't! ah, fie! 'Tis an unweeded garden
> That grows to seed; things rank and gross in nature
> Possess it merely. That it should come to this!
> But two months dead! Nay, not so much, not two.
> So excellent a king, that was to this
> Hyperion to a satyr; so loving to my mother
> That he might not beteem the winds of heaven
> Visit her face too roughly. Heaven and earth!
> Must I remember?

> But break my heart, for I must hold my tongue! [51]

Soon after, from the ghost of his father who stalks at night upon the battlements of Elsinore, he learns of his uncle's treacherous misdeed. Here again it seems as though Shakespeare were saying that the very nature of the universe is such that no wickedness can be permanently covered up. As Chaucer puts it, "Murder will out, in truth it will not fail," *The Prioress's Tale*,[52] or Jesus: "There is nothing covered, that shall not be revealed; and hid, that shall not be known." [53]

If the nature of things is such that no wicked deed can be concealed, the nature of man is such as to have misdeeds indelibly impressed upon him. So Hamlet cries to the vanished ghost who has revealed the perfidy of King Claudius and then appealed to his son's remembrance:

> Remember thee?
> Ay, thou poor ghost, while memory holds a seat
> In this distracted globe.[54]

Shakespeare goes on to present another element in the consequences of crime. It is not only a breach in the good relationships of men; it is more than an unconcealable and unforgettable fact; it also has derivatives that wreck the lives of innocent people caught up in its toils. Here emerges our belief in the solidarity of man. "No man is an Iland, intire of itselfe;" [55] as the famous passage from a devotional of John Donne has it.

In *Hamlet*, Polonius, a doddering old statesman who has served his country well but whose devices for coping with situations seem to have degenerated solely into eavesdropping, meets his death behind an arras. An innocent man becomes involved in the consequences of another's crime. Ophelia, daughter of Polonius, becomes distracted into madness over the turn of affairs. Tweedledee Rosencrantz and Tweedledum Guildenstern, one-time college friends of Hamlet, are sent to their death after being seduced into treachery. Surely here is excellent illustration of the dictum of Paul: "For none of us liveth to himself, and none dieth to himself." [56]

48

There is one further element that, through *Hamlet*, we can see in life. An evil deed never remains a single evil deed; it begets its kind, creates another, until the evildoer is destroyed by his own wickedness. Hamlet expresses it thus:

> Let it work;
> For 'tis the sport to have the engineer
> Hoist with his own petar; [57]

Laertes, too, recognizes the selfsame truth and, dying, says to Osric:

> Why, as a woodcock to mine own springe, Osric,
> I am justly kill'd with mine own treachery.[58]

See how it works out in this play. The king stealthily slays his brother and so becomes king. When he is sure the deed is suspected, he concocts knavish stratagems to cover it up. He sends Hamlet to England to be destroyed there. His plans go awry and his emissaries are destroyed instead. He rigs up a foolproof scheme whereby Laertes may most certainly kill Hamlet. And Hamlet is killed, but not until Laertes, too, is mortally wounded and Queen Gertrude is poisoned, and he himself has fallen a victim to his own craftiness, for

> Those who inflict must suffer, for they see
> The work of their own hearts and this must be
> Our chastisement or recompense— [59]

So wrote Shelley, reflecting the thought of Jesus: "and with what measure ye mete, it shall be measured unto you." [60] But the sad fact is that man does not suffer for his own evil by himself alone; the solidarity of mankind is proved in the way his evil reaches out to hurt innocent others.

Herein lies a part of the meaning of tragedy. It is not poetic justice that we find in Shakespeare. If we did, the plays would not be tragedies. Almost without exception we have, in novels, happy endings. There, often, evil meets its grim reward, and goodness finds its joyous recompense, and all are satisfied. But in Shakespeare we have no such rosy philosophy. He faced the facts that our helter-skelter life presented him with, and because of it we cannot purr at the close like Edgar's cat. Juliet and Romeo die; Lear and Cordelia suffer; Desdemona and Othello are victims of the hate of Iago. Shakespeare never gives us little answers to great questions, and he never leaves us purring. If he were to do that, he would be false to life and its high tragedy, which never leaves us without the mystery of a Cross. Our lives are intermeshed together in this reticulated world, and our wickedness, though ultimately self-defeating, brings suffering upon many.

A passage from the Second Book of Chronicles in description of Uzziah, King of Judah in the Eighth Century before Christ, aptly characterizes *Macbeth*. "His name spread far abroad; for he was marvellously helped, till he was strong. But when he was strong, his heart was lifted up to his destruction: for he transgressed." [61] Here is the sin of proud ambition or, as Macbeth himself put it:

> Vaulting ambition, which o'erleaps itself
> And falls on th' other side.[62]

Macbeth, unsatisfied with the honors that have swarmed upon him, meets the witches, the three weird sisters, who bring to light the unlawful hopes he has hitherto harbored with: "All hail, Macbeth, that shalt be King hereafter!" [63]

Lady Macbeth acts as the spur "to prick the sides of my [his] intent." [64] She recognizes that her husband is "too full o' th' milk of human kindness to catch the nearest way" [65] to carry through a plan of murdering King Duncan. That night the king is to stay at the castle Inverness; it is the opportune time; she will play on Macbeth to make him do the deed.

50

Macbeth was endowed with a strong imagination. He could picture vividly all the unlovely consequences of the deed he contemplated. Clearly he saw that events do not end with the commission of them. Alone, he listens to his conscience as it speaks through his imagination:

> If it were done when 'tis done, then 'twere well
> It were done quickly. If th' assassination
> Could trammel up the consequence, and catch,
> With his surcease, success; that but this blow
> Might be the be-all and the end-all here,
> But here, upon this bank and shoal of time,
> We'd jump the life to come. But in these cases
> We still have judgment here, that we but teach
> Bloody instructions, which, being taught, return
> To plague th' inventor. This even-handed justice
> Commends th' ingredience of our poison'd chalice
> To our own lips. He's here in double trust:
> First, as I am his kinsman and his subject—
> Strong both against the deed; then, as his host,
> Who should against his murtherer shut the door,
> Not bear the knife myself. Besides, this Duncan
> Hath borne his faculties so meek, hath been
> So clear in his great office, that his virtues
> Will plead like angels, trumpet-tongu'd, against
> The deep damnation of his taking-off;
> And pity, like a naked new-born babe,
> Striding the blast, or heaven's cherubin, hors'd
> Upon the sightless couriers of the air,
> Shall blow the horrid deed in every eye,
> That tears shall drown the wind. I have no spur
> To prick the sides of my intent, but only
> Vaulting ambition, which o'erleaps itself
> And falls on th' other side.[66]

Then Lady Macbeth takes him in hand. Her ambition seems to be centered in him, as though she wants nothing for herself. She has resolved that he shall be what the Weird Sisters have promised him. She has prayed:

> Come, you spirits
> That tend on mortal thoughts, unsex me here,
> And take my milk for gall,[67]

that she might see the deed well done. Therefore, when her husband announces to her his resolve to give up the notion of slaying Duncan, to "proceed no further in this business," [68] because he does not want to lose the "golden opinions" [69] he has bought "from all sorts of people," [70] she is ready for him:

> Art thou afeard
> To be the same in thine own act and valour
> As thou art in desire? Wouldst thou have that
> Which thou esteem'st the ornament of life,
> And live a coward in thine own esteem,
> Letting 'I dare not' wait upon 'I would,'
> Like the poor cat i' the adage? [71]

Her thrust strikes home. "Prithee peace!" [72] he cries:

> I dare do all that may become a man,
> Who dares do more is none.[73]

Lady Macbeth succeeds with her "undaunted mettle," [74] dismissing all thought of failure with an incredulous, "we fail?" [75]

When the castle is quiet and its inhabitants asleep, Macbeth sees the famous "dagger of the mind:" [76]

> Is this a dagger which I see before me,
> The handle toward my hand? Come, let me clutch thee!
> I have thee not, and yet I see thee still.
> Art thou not, fatal vision, sensible

52

To feeling as to sight? or art thou but
A dagger of the mind, a false creation,
Proceeding from the heat-oppressed brain?
I see thee yet, in form as palpable
As this which now I draw.
Thou marshall'st me the way that I was going,
And such an instrument I was to use.
Mine eyes are made the fools o' th' other senses,
Or else worth all the rest. I see thee still;
And on thy blade and dudgeon gouts of blood,
Which was not so before. There's no such thing.
It is the bloody business which informs
Thus to mine eyes.[77]

It is the symbolic dagger of violence, of ruthless force, that,
red with blood, gets what it can and keeps what it can hold.

There is, for one who thinks of Jesus, an ominous quality
in the scene. "All who take the sword will perish by the
sword." [78] And this scene may well stand as the death knell
of the spirit of Macbeth—and of his body. Certainly it meant
woe and war for Scotland. It is a vivid warning to nations,
too, who take up the sword which "marshall'st me [them]
the way that I [they] was [were] going" [79]—toward destruction.

Furthermore, Macbeth recognizes at this time the sympathy of nature with goodness and its antagonism against
those who bring havoc into human affairs. He addresses the
earth:

Thou sure and firm-set earth,
Hear not my steps which way they walk, for fear
The very stones prate of my whereabout.[80]

Macbeth, when the time has come and his wife has
struck upon the bell, cries,

I go, and it is done. The bell invites me.
Hear it not, Duncan, for it is a knell
That summons thee to heaven, or to hell.[81]

One must delve deep to plumb the depths of Shakespeare.
Nowhere in our literature, I suspect, is the power of conscience more superbly pictured than in the scenes following
the king's murder. Macbeth is distracted when he comes
down the stairs. A part of the scene reads:

Macbeth. I have done the deed. Didst thou not hear a noise?
Lady M. I heard the owl scream and the cricket cry.
      Did not you speak?
Macbeth. Methought I heard a voice cry 'Sleep no more!
      Macbeth does murther sleep.'—the innocent sleep,
      Sleep that knits up the ravell'd sleave of care,
      The death of each day's life, sore labour's bath,
      Balm of hurt minds, great nature's second course,
      Chief nourisher in life's feast.[82]

One of the most profound touches of the drama is just
here. Macbeth has heard the youngsters asking God to bless
them, and he cannot say Amen. Here he is awakened to the
consciousness of guilt through the discovery that he cannot
say that word.

                   I stood and heard them
But they did say their prayers and address'd them
Again to sleep. . . .
One cried 'God bless us!' and 'Amen!' the other,
As they had seen me with these hangman's hands,
List'ning their fear. I could not say 'Amen!'
When they did say 'God bless us!' . . .
But wherefore could not I pronounce 'Amen'?
I had most need of blessing, and 'Amen'

Stuck in my throat.[83]

54

"Be sure your sin will find you out." [84] Note how that goes, and how Shakespeare seems to illustrate it. It is not merely that your sin will necessarily be found out, for Macbeth's enemies do not oppose him because they know of all his perfidy, but it will find you out. Already we can see Macbeth reeling under the impact of this terrible deed. "I could not [he cannot] say Amen" [85] though he has "most need of blessing"; [86] he cannot sleep henceforth; his sins has found him out.

As with King Claudius of Denmark, so it is with Macbeth, now King of Scotland. Fortune has been with him up to this point. "He was marvelously helped, till he was strong. But when he was strong, his heart was lifted up to his destruction." [87] Lady Macbeth formulates it another way, but it is the same idea: "What need we fear who knows it, when none can call our pow'r to accompt?" [88] But the consciousness of guilt, of transgression against a trust and against a moral law, weighs heavily upon his mind. So, like King Claudius, he wades more deeply into blood. Banquo is his next victim, then still others, until all Scotland is steeped in blood.

Here again is the familiar truth of our solidarity. In the exigencies of life, Shakespeare came upon it. When one man sins, the effects thereof are not confined to himself. I repeat that Shakespeare does not give us poetic justice. Not Macbeth alone, but others must suffer for his ambitious crime. Banquo died, Lady Macduff and her children perished, and the whole of Scotland was seethed in blood. It is difficult to think of a more forceful example of the unity of mankind.

Out of his consciousness of guilt, Macbeth brings ruin to himself. Lady Macbeth, too, suffers for her denial of her human self. She steels herself to spur Macbeth after he has killed the king. She blandly says:

> Go get some water
> And wash this filthy witness from your hand.

A little water clears us of this deed.[89]

But her mind nonetheless becomes infected with the crime. Macbeth is right, not she, about the washing away of the evidences of the blood from their hands. He has said:

> Will all great Neptune's ocean wash this blood
> Clean from my hand? No. This my hand will rather
> The multitudinous seas incarnadine,
> Making the green one red.[90]

She later walks in her sleep, piteously sighing and rubbing her hands:

> Out, damned spot; out, I say!

> Here's the smell of the blood still. All the perfumes
> of Arabia will not sweeten this little hand.[91]

It is the dramatic touch of the Gospel that shows us Pontius Pilate vainly washing his hands, and coupled with the fatal remorse of Judas Iscariot.

As for Macbeth, the "golden opinions" [92] which he had bought "from all sorts of people" [93] turns to their hatred. He has grasped the dagger to secure the throne; he wields the sword to make the throne secure; but through it all he finds no security:

> O, full of scorpions is my mind, dear wife! [94]

He has lamented, and:

> Naught's had, all's spent,
> When our desire is got without content.[95]

That same dagger which he had earlier seen before his eyes, and "on thy [its] blade and dudgeon gouts of blood." [96] has been prophetic. It is wielded against him by Macduff whose life he has sought. No appealing to the weird witches, like the other monarch, **Saul, at the c**ave of Endor, can save

Macbeth. He takes refuge in their deceptive prophecies, but Birnam wood moves up to Dunsinane, like Abimelech and his army to the tower of Shechem,[97] and one not normally born of woman grasps the sword that takes his life.

It is Nemesis indeed. "It will have blood, they say; blood will have blood." [98] Macbeth had said this to his Lady, seeing clearly the nature of the retribution that awaited him. Emerson puts it differently: "Nemesis is that recoil of Nature, not to be guarded against, which ever surprises the most wary transgressor." [99]

> This even-handed justice
> Commends th' ingredience of our poison'd chalice
> To our [his] own lips.[100]

John Erskine, in a notable chapter in his *Delight of Great Books*, says that *The Tempest, A Winter's Tale*, and *Cymbeline*, Shakespeare's last three plays, are pictures of life problems. Life, he says, is a troubled adventure in which "a kind of inner retribution at last justifies the good and the wise, and exposes the wicked and the mistaken." [101] It may be well, then, to turn to one of the final plays, *The Tempest*, to see how this "kind of inner retribution" [102] works out.

Prospero, in action antecedent to the opening of the drama, had been the Duke of Milan. However, he was not interested overly much in political affairs; he rather centered his attention in his books; state matters were left in the hands of his brother, Antonio. Invested with the reality of power, Antonio wanted the appearance of it, too, so he usurped the dukedom, causing his bookish brother to be exiled. Prospero and his daughter, Miranda, were set adrift in a little boat. By good fortune, they made their way to an island. Although its location is not very clear, it appears to have been in the Mediterranean. There Prospero continued to study his books and practice the magic he found in them. He became supreme on the island; even half-human creatures like Caliban and spirits like Ariel submitted to his will.

The play opens with a storm at sea and a shipwreck, events induced by Prospero's magic. His brother, the usurping duke, is one of those on board. The entire shipwrecked company eventually come before Prospero and the old wrongs are righted, the good and wise are justified and the wicked and mistaken exposed.

Before the ultimate unwinding of the plot, however, Shakespeare shows again the way in which evil continues to reproduce itself in more evil. Antonio, the usurping Duke, plots with Sebastian, son of the king of Naples who is also a member of the shipwrecked party, to usurp the Naples throne. Here again is the vicious circle that pride and violence and power-grasping sets up. This plot is foiled by Prospero's magic. Here we have, in what was likely the last of Shakespeare's plays, the theme of one of his earliest tragedies, *Romeo and Juliet*. There the violence of the Capulets and Montagues created more violence and threatened to undo the city-state. Here the violence likewise has its social and political results. In *Romeo and Juliet* harmony came finally because of love, but the solution was tragic. In *The Tempest* harmony was restored in the state and among individuals through goodwilled wisdom that had become powerful.

Prospero gets his revenge on his enemies, but it is merciful revenge. "The noblest vengeance is to forgive," [103] or, as the play puts it:

> The rarer action is
> In virtue [i.e., mercy] than in vengeance.[104]

He says to Antonio:

> For you, most wicked sir, whom to call brother
> Would even infect my mouth, I do forgive
> Thy rankest fault—all of them; and require
> My dukedom of thee, which perforce I know
> Thou must restore.[105]

The final scene presents a speech of old Gonzalo's wherein he summarizes the situations of the major characters. Ferdinand, son of the king of Naples, has fallen in love with Miranda, daughter of the now-restored Duke of Milan; Prospero has come back into his own; but most important of all, this "inner retribution" [106] has restored everyone to his true self.

> Was Milan thrust from Milan that his issue
> Should become kings of Naples? O, rejoice
> Beyond a common joy, and set it down
> With gold on lasting pillars: In one voyage
> Did Claribel her husband find at Tunis,
> And Ferdinand her brother found a wife
> Where he himself was lost; Prospero his dukedom
> In a poor isle; and all of us ourselves
> When no man was his own.[107]

Even Caliban has found, by his idolizing a foolish human, that foolishness turned in upon him. Stephano and Trinculo turned out to be rather inadequate as gods. He is restored to his better senses, and will never again, he says, worship man.

> I'll be wise hereafter,
> And seek for grace. What a thrice-double ass
> Was I to take this drunkard for a god
> And worship this dull fool! [108]

But Prospero is our main concern. He was a victim of injustice, but he does not return injustice again; he remains strong, brave, untouched by ill-will, faithful to himself and the wisdom of his books. All things, for him at least, work together for good. One thinks of Browning's line: "For sudden the worst turns the best to the brave." [109] Is Shakespeare saying that book-wisdom—and the magic there is in books—may not at first rule men who are violent and proud?

Rather, he seems to say, the proud and power-loving will drive the wisdom-lovers away to exile. Look to *Measure for Measure:*

> But man, proud man,
> Drest in a little brief authority,
> Most ignorant of what he's most assur'd
> (His glassy essence), like an angry ape,
> Plays such fantastic tricks before high heaven
> As make the angels weep; [100]

But weeping angels and proud men with little authority are not the last word. Rather, that last word lies with wisdom that uses power well, with Prospero. He, the learner, the meek, became regnant and saved the state. Here is meek man, the wise and mighty meek, "the terrible meek," [111] inheriting the earth.

One other element in *The Tempest* needs to be pointed out. It was this same Prospero who said,

> We are such stuff
> As dreams are made on, and our little life
> Is rounded with a sleep.[112]

Indeed Prospero was the dreamer, and the interpreter of the dreams of others in a profound sense. Here we come upon the Joseph theme, as presented in Genesis. Joseph, like Prospero, was exiled: his brothers came to him where he was in great power; he ministered to them, though they did not know him at first; and he forgave them. Again, "The noblest vengeance is to forgive." [113] Maybe it is only this, between nations and amongst men, that can give us hope, and that will make us exclaim with Miranda:

> O brave new world
> That has such people in't! [114]

Perhaps it would be well to end this chapter with a sonnet composed by E. K. Chambers, the magnificent Shakespearean scholar, on the man Shakespeare himself. For our author was the recipient of his justice, too. He looked into the hearts of men and wrote of what he came upon there. With deep insight into man's fantastic brain, he smiled gaily at first, then sadly, and serenely at the last, leaving us wise and sane. So Chambers wrote of him:

I like to think of Shakespeare, not as when
In our old London of the spacious time
He took all amorous hearts with honeyed rhyme;
Or flung his jest at Burbage and at Ben;
Or speared the flying follies with his pen;
Or, in deep hour, made Juliet's love sublime;
Or from Lear's kindness and Iago's crime
Caught tragic hint of heaven's dark way with men.
These were great memories, but he laid them down.
And when, with brow composed and friendly tread,
He sought the little streets of Stratford town,
That knew his dreams and soon must hold him dead,
   I like to think how Shakespeare pruned his rose,
   And ate his pippin in his orchard close.[115]

Notes *

1. George Lyman Kittredge (ed.), *The Complete Works of Shakespeare*, (Boston: Ginn & Company, 1936), *Macbeth*, Act I, Scene vii, Line 10.
2. *Ibid.*
3. *Ibid.*, *King Henry V*, Act II, Scene III, Line 15.

* With the exception of quotations reprinted from works in the public domain all excerpts are used by special permission of the present copyright holders.

4. G. H. Palmer, *Intimations of Immortality in the Sonnets of Shakespere*, (Boston: Houghton Mifflin Co., 1912), pp. 50 and 51.

5. *Ibid.*, pp. 50 and 51.

6. *Ibid.*, pp. 51 and 52.

7. *Ibid.*, p. 51.

8. Kittredge, *op. cit.*, *King Lear*, Act I, Scene ii, Lines 128—138.

9. *Ibid.*, Act IV, Scene iii, Lines 34 and 35.

10. *Ibid.*, Scene i, Lines 36 and 37.

11. *Ibid.*, Scene ii, Lines 79, 80 and 81.

12. *Ibid.*, Act V, Scene iii, Lines 302, 303 and 304.

13. *Ibid.*, Act IV, Scene vi, Lines 73 and 74.

14. *Ibid.*, Act V, Scene iii, Lines 170 and 171.

15. *Ibid.*, *Hamlet*, Act V, Scene ii, Lines 10 and 11.

16. *Holy Bible*, K.J.V., Judges 5:20.

17. Kittredge, *op. cit.*, *King John*, Act IV, Scene ii, Lines 182 to 202.

18. *Ibid.*, *Julius Caesar*, Act II, Scene ii, Lines 17ff.

19. *Ibid.*, *Macbeth*, Act II, Scene iv, Lines 4ff.

20. Frank W. Cody and Van H. Cartmell (editors) *Shakespeare Arranged For Modern Reading*. (Garden City, New York), *Lear*, Act III, Scene i, p. 957.

21. Kittredge, *op. cit.*, *Julius Caesar*, Act I, Scene ii, Line 194.

22. *Ibid.*, Lines 139 to 141.

23. Karl A. Menninger, *Man Against Himself*, (New York: Harcourt, Brace and Co., 1938).

24. Kittredge, *op. cit.*, *Titus Andronicus*, Act V, Scene iii, Lines 201 and 202.

25. *Holy Bible*, K.J.V., Hosea 8:7.

26. Mark Van Doren, *Shakespeare*, (New York: Henry Holt & Co., 1939), p. 44.

27. *Holy Bible*, K.J.V., I Cor. 1:27.

28. Homer, *The Iliad*, trans. W. B. Smith and W. Miller (New York: The Macmillan Co., 1945), Bk. XXII.

29. Kittredge, *op. cit.*, *Merchant of Venice*, Act II, Scene viii, Lines 12-21.

30. *Holy Bible*, K.J.V., Genesis 31:36.

31. Kittredge, *op. cit.*, *Merchant of Venice*, Act I, Scene iii, Lines 72ff.

32. *Ibid.*, Act I, Scene iii, Lines 107-130.

33. *Ibid.*, Act III, Scene i, Lines 55-76.

34. *Holy Bible*, K.J.V., Exodus 21:24.

35. *Ibid.*, Matthew 5:38.

36. *Ibid.*, 5:39.

37. *Ibid.*, Deuteronomy 32:35 and Hebrews 10:30.

38. Kittredge, *op. cit.*, *Merchant of Venice*, Act IV, Scene i, Lines 184-202.

39. *Ibid.*, Line 396.

40. *Holy Bible*, K.J.V., Proverbs 26:27.

41. Kittredge, *op. cit.*, *Romeo and Juliet*, *Prologue* Line 6.

42. *Ibid.*, Lines 1-11.

43. *Ibid.*, Act I, Scene i, Lines 96-104.

44. *Ibid.*, Act II, Scene ii, Line 118.

45. *The Holy Bible*, A.R.S. (New York: Thomas Nelson & Sons, 1901), I Cor. 13:8.

46. Kittredge, *op. cit.*, *Romeo and Juliet*, Act V, Scene iii, Lines 291-295.

47. *The Holy Bible*, A.R.S. Mark 3:23.

48. *Ibid.*, Matthew 5:44.

49. Kittredge, *op. cit.*, *Romeo and Juliet*, Act V, Scene ii, Line 296.

50. *The Holy Bible*, A.R.S., Ecclesiastes 1:2.

51. Kittredge, *op cit.*, *Hamlet*, Act I, Scene ii, Lines 129ff.

52. Chaucer's *Canterbury Tales*, An Interlinear Translation by Vincent F. Hopper, Brooklyn, N. Y. Barron's Educational Series, Inc., 1948, p. 208, Line 89.

53. *The Holy Bible*, A.R.S., Matthew 10:26.

54. Kittredge, *op. cit.*, *Hamlet*, Act I, Scene v, Lines 95-97.

55. Christopher Morley (ed.), John Bartlett's Familiar Quotations. (Boston: Little, Brown & Co., 1948), John Donne's Devotions, XVII Line 1, p. 1039.

56. *The Holy Bible*, A.R.S., Romans 14:7.

57. Kittredge, *op. cit.*, *Hamlet*, Act III, Scene iv, Lines 205-207.

58. *Ibid.*, Act V, Scene ii, Lines 317-318.

59. Harry Buxton Forman (ed.), *The Works of Percy Bysshe Shelley* in 8 Vols., (London: Reeves & Turner, 1880.), Third Vol., Poetry III, p. 124, *Julian and Maddalo*, Lines 482-483-484.

60. *The Holy Bible*, A.R.S., Matthew 7:2.

61. *Holy Bible*, K.J.V., II Chronicles 26:15b-16a.

62. Kittredge, *op. cit.*, *Macbeth*, Act I, Scene vii, Lines 27-28.

63. *Ibid.*, Scene iii, Line 50.

64. *Ibid.*, Scene vii., Line 26.

65. *Ibid.*, Scene v, Lines 18-19.

66. *Ibid.*, Scene vii, Lines 1-28.

67. *Ibid.*, Scene v, Lines 41-42-49.

68. *Ibid.*, Scene vii, Line 31.

69. *Ibid.*, Line 33.

70. *Ibid.*

71. *Ibid.*, Lines 39-44.

72. *Ibid.*, Line 45.

73. *Ibid.*, Lines 46-47.

74. *Ibid.*, Line 74.

75. *Ibid.*, Scene vii, Line 59.

76. *Ibid.*, Act II, Scene i, Line 38.

77. *Ibid.*, Lines 33-49.

78. *The New Testament*, R.S.V. New York: Thomas Nelson & Sons. Copyrighted 1946 and 1942 by the Division of Christian Education of the National Council of Churches and used by permission. Matthew 26:52.

79. Kittredge, *op. cit.*, *Macbeth*, Act II, Scene i, Line 42.

80. *Ibid.*, Lines 56-58.

81. *Ibid.*, Lines 62-64.

82. *Ibid.*, Scene ii, Lines 15-40.

83. *Ibid.*, Lines 24-33.

84. *Holy Bible*, K.J.V., Numbers 32:23.

85. Kittredge, *op. cit.*, *Macbeth*, Act II, Scene ii, Line 28.

86. *Ibid.*, Line 32.

87. *Holy Bible*, K.J.V., II Chronicles 26:15b-16a.

88. Kittredge, *op. cit.*, *Macbeth*, Act V, Scene i, Line 42.

89. *Ibid.*, Act II, Scene ii, Lines 46-47-67.

90. *Ibid.*, Lines 60-63.

91. *Ibid.*, Act V, Scene i, Lines 39-56-58.

92. *Ibid.*, Act I, Scene vii, Line 33.

93. *Ibid.*

94. *Ibid.*, Act III, Scene ii, Line 36.

95. *Ibid.*, Lines 4-5.

96. *Ibid.*, Act II, Scene i, Line 46.

97. *Holy Bible*, K.J.V., Judges 9:48-49.

98. Kittredge, *op. cit.*, *Macbeth*, Act III, Scene iv, Line 122.

99. E. W. Emerson & W. E. Forbes (ed.) *Journals of Ralph Waldo Emerson* 1820-1876 in 10 Vols. (Boston: Houghton Mifflin Co., 1914) Vol. X, p. 76.

100. Kittredge, *op. cit.*, *Macbeth*, Act I, Scene vii, Lines 9-11.

101. John Erskine, *The Delight of Great Books* (Indianapolis: The Bobbs-Merrill Co., 1928). p. 130.

102. *Ibid.*

103. Burton Stevenson (ed.) *The Handbook of Quotations*, (Philadelphia: The Blakiston Co., 1944), p. 1711. "The noblest vengeance is to forgive" in H. G. Bohn, *Handbook of Proverbs*, p. 512.

104. Kittredge, *op. cit.*, *The Tempest*, Act V, Scene i, Lines 27-28.

105. *Ibid.*, Lines 130-134.

106. Erskine, *op. cit.*

107. Kittredge, *op. cit.*, *The Tempest*, Act V, Scene i, Lines 205-213.

108. *Ibid.*, Lines 294-297.

109. Caroline Miles Hill (ed.), *The World's Great Religious Poetry*, (New York: Macmillan Co., 1942), p. 671. Robert Browning's "Prospice," Line 21.

110. Kittredge, *op. cit.*, *Measure for Measure*, Act II, Scene ii, Lines 117-122.

111. Charles Rann Kennedy, *The Terrible Meek*, (New York: Samuel French, 1912), p. 39.

112. Kittredge, *op. cit.*, *The Tempest*, Act IV, Scene i, Lines 156-158.

113. Burton Stevenson, *op. cit.*, p. 1711.

114. Kittredge, *op. cit.*, *The Tempest*, Act V, Scene i, Lines 184-185.

115. E. K. Chambers, *Shakespeare: A Survey*, (London: Sedgwick and Jackson Ltd., 1925), p. 325.

Chapter 3

BACKGROUNDS OF PRESENT-DAY
RELIGIOUS DRAMA

The Beginnings

From the very beginning, man has felt the need for self-expression. This first took the form of a rude ritualistic service to some unknown power or god, which he had come to believe exerted an influence over him.

Probably this urge first expressed itself in a crude form of dance, through which the early man gave voice to his prayers, and thanks to the god of his conception.

Undoubtedly, the first theatre was a dancing circle, perhaps in some sacred grove or at the foot of a hill. The noises made by the dancers, combined with rhythmic movement of the body, ultimately led to poetic expression through which the primitive man imitated victories over his enemies and his struggles against the forces of nature. We find all through religious history that the dance was accepted as a means of praise and worship. Today it is suggested and encouraged by one of the better books on the subject. Margaret Palmer Fisk discusses, in her volume entitled *The Art of the Rhythmic Choir*, the values of worship through symbolic movement.[1] Many places of worship, particularly in the eastern part of the United States, are experimenting with it today with most exciting and valuable results.

Greek and Roman Drama

The dancing instinct gave way to the playhouses of the ancient Greeks, and the magnificent theatres of the Romans. The early plays of these people were more or less of a religious spectacle, and represented the devotion of the people to their particular god or gods. However, the theatre of the Romans degenerated to such a degree that, two hundred years after the birth of Christ, there was so much viciousness and evil in their presentations that they excited the indignation, not only of the Christians, but of the better class of Romans as well.

The Roman theatre persisted through the fifth and into the sixth century, and then died in the bitter conflict with Christianity which was constantly growing more and more powerful.

Roman Catholic Drama

The love of acting was so ingrained in the human soul that it could not be stifled, and as a result, after the decline of the Roman theatre, wandering actors were seen producing scraps of old plays in courts, festivals, and in city streets. Then followed the traveling reader, going from place to place, from home to home, reciting poetical stories and entrancing his auditors. In the ninth century the priests of the Roman Catholic Church conceived the idea of inserting a song with words into the mass. In this the church sought to portray religious faith more vividly by means of impersonators, instead of having only one person intone the incident in Latin, which very few understood. So popular did this form of religious inspiration become that it was not long before there appeared dramatic representations of religious events such as the Last Supper, the Angel at the Sepulchre, the Three Marys at the Tomb of Jesus, and many other religious incidents.

From the tenth century to the thirteenth, we find the

Latin text gradually changing to a mixture of Latin and the vernacular, and finally to French, German, and other tongues.

The singing or chanting ultimately gave way to a group or series of incidents until the Easter Group had enough incidents for a Passion Play, the Christmas Group for a Nativity Play, and the Ascension Group for a Resurrection Play. So popular were those plays with the public that the actors became more bold in interpreting their theme, so that as an empty tomb and the three Marys were presented, one of the Marys would hold up to view the castoff burial clothing as proof that Jesus had left the tomb.

The Mysteries, The Miracles, and The Moralities

These mystery plays, as they came to be called, found in church edifices an appropriate and very beautiful setting. The Birth of Jesus, the Adoration of the Shepherds, the Three Wise Men, Herod, and the Slaughter of the Innocents furnished ample material for the building up of crude religious dramas, which pictured to an illiterate people those scenes and incidents which formed the basis for religious belief. These mystery plays grew more elaborate and the church edifices were not large enough to hold all who wished to witness them, so simple stages were built outside of the church.

There never was a good thing in the world that wasn't mimicked, and it was not long before the lower clergy, who were actors in the miracle plays, introduced burlesques of the various miracle and mystery plays, as well as dramatic humorous presentations of church services, embodying various caricatures of priests and bishops.

Vigorous opposition was aroused and just as it took the early Fathers of the Christian Church almost three hundred years to drive the actors from the disgusting stages of Rome, so in the Middle Ages it took them three hundred years to rid the houses of God of semi-theatrical desecrations.

Thus we see that serious religious drama originated in the

mass, out of which grew the mystery and miracle plays which were originally performed at the church altar. The passion plays of today, for example, are an evolution of the miracle and mystery plays of the Middle Ages.

The usual division of the productions of the Medieval religious drama is made into three classes. The mysteries proper deal wtih scriptural events only, and set forth, with the aid of the prophetic history of the Old Testament and the fulfilling events of the New, the central mystery of the Redemption of the world, as accomplished by the Nativity, the Passion and the Resurrection. These were not kept distinctly apart from the miracle plays, or miracles, which are strictly speaking concerned with the legends of the saints. The moralities, or moral plays, teach and illustrate the same truths allegorically, their characters being personified virtues or qualities. *Everyman*, perhaps the most perfect example of its class, contains passages certainly designed to enforce the specific teaching of Rome. Dowden in his *Introduction to Shakespeare* explains the growth of drama and its fruition in the arrival of Shakespeare upon the scene when he tells us:

The moment was especially a fortunate one for a dramatic writer. The development of every art during its earlier stages is gradual and slow; the bud insensibly swells and matures, then suddenly some genial morning the calyx bursts, the bud becomes a blossom, and all its colour and fragrance are open to the day. So it was with the dramatic art in the later Elizabethan years. Its history from the earliest miracle plays had been one of some centuries. The drama was not the creation of a few eminent individuals, but rather a product of the national mind distinguished by the features of the national character. In the Collective Mystery, which surveyed the history of the human race from the origin of man to the judgment day, it had gained an epic breadth. In the Moralities it had acquired an ethical depth, a seriousness of moral purpose,

70

and this didactic tendency had in a measure been saved from the aridity and abstractedness of mere allegory by the close connection of the Morality with historical passions, persons, and events. In both the Miracles and the Moralities scope had been found for the play of humor, sometimes deliberately sought as a relief from the poetry of edification, sometimes naively mingling with passages of grace, tenderness, or pathos, and enhancing the effect of these.[2]

Thus came the great masterpieces of Shakespeare, whose therapeutic value we discussed earlier. Later came the ethical plays of Ibsen and the great dramas of George Bernard Shaw.

Notes *

1. Margaret Palmer Fisk, *The Art of the Rhythmic Choir*, (New York: Harper and Brothers, 1950).

2. Edward Dowden, *Introduction to Shakespeare*, (New York: Charles Scribner's Sons, n.d.), pp. 44-45.

3. Material on the Medieval Period, in addition to direct quotes, was suggested by the article on: "Drama," *Encyclopaedia Britannica*, Vol. VII, (1952).

PART II

THERAPEUTIC VALUES IN THE USE OF
DRAMA AND THE DRAMATIC
IN THE CHURCH

Chapter 1

THE THERAPEUTICS OF WORSHIP

Introduction

How is Worship Expressed?

We find that worship expresses itself in different ways. Three of these ways are important for our interest and understanding:

First, there is the factor of adoration. Man finds himself in the presence of such wonder and beauty in the world that instinctively he bows himself in humility and awe. This prostration of body and mind involves no element of superstition. Man is not frightened or deceived. The world is real and it is good and so is the pageantry of nature as real and good as man's instinctive reaction to its splendor. Take the stars, for example! Can man be expected to stand unmoved before the majestic procession of the heavens? Must he not rather lift his hands in ecstasy or bow his head in humility? Emerson has answered this question in his essay on "Nature," where he says, "If the stars should appear one night in a thousand years, how would men believe and adore; and preserve for many generations the remembrance of the city of God which had been shown!" [1]

The second element of worship to which we now come is what we call communion by which we mean the personal contact of man with the world in which he lives.

To make this clear is difficult, and yet how true it is. In his great poem, "Thanatopsis," written when he was only nineteen years of age, the American poet, William Cullen Bryant, addresses him who

> . . . in the love of Nature holds
> Communion with her visible forms . . .[2]

Just what the poet means by this "communion"[3] with nature is hard to say. But in some of the greater human spirits we find a contact between the outer and inner life which may well be described as "communion."[4] Thus, Pythagoras, the ancient philosopher, was so impressed with the harmony of the universe, the sweet accord of part with part, that he claimed there was a music of the spheres which man could hear in his deeper moments of humility and apprehension and to which he could give answer in the music of his own soul. It is something more than a legend or folk tale that when Henry Thoreau tramped the woods of Concord, the wild creatures did not flee him but, on the contrary, came to him, and even the fishes, as he knelt by the water-side, swam to him to be caressed by his gentle hand. This is what we mean by communion. There is a communion of man with spirit, a divine element which flows about him and catches up his deep longings for higher things—a humble companionship with all that lives—a reaching forth of man's inner life toward that which fills the world as water fills the stream in which it flows. It is this communion of humility which comes to us most nearly in our hours of worship. This worship may take various forms. These forms run all the way from the humble simplicities of the Quaker meeting to the pomp and ceremony of the Roman Mass. They may include no church, but only man humble and alone with nature and his own soul. But they all are aimed, these forms of worship, at this communion of which we speak. Thus man humbly seeks God— to find him where he may be found. So worship has to do with communion as well as with adoration.

We now come to a third and final aspect of worship. How to describe this, we do not know. We cannot think of any single word to serve our purpose. Worship, in its deepest implications, is an attempt to enlarge our lives and lift them to high places. As it is, these lives of ours are all too limited and are active on too low a level. We are beset within by baser sentiments and fears and without by the bounds and barriers of our world. Constantly we reach far for the shining horizons of the soul, only to find ourselves checked at the point where we stand. What we need is a consciousness within us of the infinite and external—to "enlarge the place of thy [our] tent," as Isaiah puts it, "to stretch forth the curtains of thine [our] habitations: . . . to lengthen thy [our] cords and strengthen thy [our] stakes." [5] And this is what worship does for us! Not always, for we are "groundlings," [6] as Shakespeare reminds us! But there come moments when we are worshipping in silence and alone or moments when we are lifting our voices with the great congregation that we feel ourselves possessed by a power greater than ourselves. This is worship working for us its miracle of enlargement, of elevation, of expansion, so that, without understanding how it happens, we become greater than ourselves.

Such is worship in the true sense of the world. It is *adoration* as we stand in humility and awe before the magic and mystery of this world which is our home. It is humble *communion* with the living spirit which wraps us 'round like the very atmosphere we feel and breathe. It is *enlargement* of our inner faculties, our spiritual stature, to meet and work with God. Hence the emotional attitudes aroused by the services of the churches are the tender, melting moods in which the will acquiesces in the appeal for love and comradeship.

The importance of true worship was emphasized by Washington Gladden when he stated: "As the Protestant church of today is seeking to become a working church, so, and for kindred reasons, it is seeking to be a worshipping church." [7] Dr. Robinson pointedly asks himself the question: "How does the church most securely receive the guidance of God and realize her divine character?" [8] In reply he says:

I would claim that two things are necessary: (a) the attitude of worship and (b) that she should be under the judgment of the word of God. If the real basis of worship is communion or fellowship—fellowship with God in Christ and with one another—then the church will most fully realize and actualize her divine character in worship.[9]

The thought is further encouraged by the authors of *Religious Radio: What to Do and How* when they say:

Deep within the heart of man is an imperishable hunger for fellowship. Deep within him, also, is an imperishable vision and conviction of the essential oneness of man. The realization that one-world living is a new dimension of life for all the sons and daughters of Adam is upon us and we wonder what that new life is. What essential service can be rendered man today by a church which will lift up, dramatize, celebrate, put forward these imperishable yearnings, dreams, actualities! [10]

further:

The assumption of Protestant worship is that each worshiper must worship. Worship is not the minister offering up something in our place and for us. It is rather that the words and music of the service open the heart of the listener so that he and God will commune with each other, and he will no longer resist the work of God.[11]

and:

The human matrix of worship is a community of purpose and loyalty; a fellowship group whose fate and life are celebrated in communal worship. Unless this is present in reality or in strong imagination worship is not full-bodied.[12]

With a knowledge of how worship is expressed we turn to the elements of it which will encourage a therapy worthy to be called Christian and endeavor to direct our thinking to those values inherent in the use of drama and the dramatic in the Church.

Preaching

All religious bodies agree the preaching of the gospel must have its due honor. Preaching is not the center of worship but it can be the dramatic touch which makes the gospel's message helpful. The worship thus becomes "spontaneous dramatic action" producing a "catharsis in spontaneity."

For example, J. S. Whale in his volume *Christian Doctrine* tells us: "Thus, in the full diet of public worship in every Church throughout Christendom, two permanent elements together constitute 'the means of grace';" [13] and he notes as the "first, the preaching and hearing of the Word." [14]

In an article in *Pastoral Psychology* under the title, "The Therapeutic Function in Preaching," Edgar N. Jackson writes: "The use of the sermon as an instrument of group therapy is probably one of the oldest forms of ministry to the soul needs of mankind." [15] Further he states: "The finest examples of preaching as a soul healing force came from the ministry of Jesus." [16]

With these thoughts in mind let us turn to our topic and observe the preacher as he dramatizes the truth he is presenting. While we will be discussing the Sermon on the Mount, as the material of Jesus, a little later, it will appear now and then as we concern ourselves with his personality as the preacher.

At the time of preaching, the personality of the preacher —his human quality and character—is undoubtedly a pronounced vital element in making the impression produced by the message. Today the human element contributes greatly to the immediate impression and success made by an orator. Ordinary thinking, commonplace opinions, a thoroughly conventionalized literary style, sometimes produce amazing effects under the magical spell of the orator's magnetic personality. It is what Dean Brown means when he says:

> In the preaching of a real sermon the whole man is acting and reacting under the stimulus offered by the spiritual needs of a body of people. The preacher's face and bearing, his voice and his eye, all his mental faculties—reason, judgment, insight, imagination and the rest—all his spiritual faculties—sympathy, aspiration, high resolve, faith, hope and love—all these are engaged in a concerted movement upon the minds and hearts of those listeners.[17]

It is afterwards, when the words appear in cold print—when there are no thrilling tone colors and impassioned gestures to inflame the imagination and quicken the emotions—that the actual quality of what has been said is found to be worth something or merely twaddle. Will the spoken words stand calm reading and cool analysis when the intelligence is no longer more or less somnolent under the orator's personal appeal? This is the real test of the genuine thought content.

It is not necessary to argue the unwarrantedness and unreasonableness of the orthodox Christian claim that Jesus is God himself. Jesus never taught it. It is clearly one of the byproducts of ecclesiasticism. The deification of Jesus is the gravest misfortune that has befallen Christians. It has made those who have accepted it worshippers of a human personality instead of what they should be, demonstrators of a living truth.

The real danger for the preacher or teacher here is that as he dramatizes the truth he is presenting he becomes the incarnation of that truth. When mankind places a halo on any human being—something it is lamentably prone to do with those who have been the preachers or teachers of advancing religious thought and freedom—it forthwith begins to devote itself to the aggrandizement of the messenger's personality. By the same token it neglects and in time almost completely loses sight of the true value and meaning of the message. Sentimental devotion to the person takes the place of an understanding of what the person was trying to teach and practice. To proclaim the infallibility of the preacher is deemed greater loyalty than to follow the preacher's example by opening fresh vistas of enlarging service to humanity.

Christians say that Jesus is their Way-Shower. By that do they mean that what he did, they can learn to do—that they can learn to live the life of mental and spiritual might that he lived? "Greater works than these shall he [that believeth in me] do," [18] he said, though the theological claim that Jesus is God makes it impossible to believe that Jesus meant what he said when he said it.

If Jesus were not a human being like the rest of us, if our problems of nature, character, temperament, disposition, limitation, were not his problems, if he did not face temptations like ours and overcome weaknesses similar to our weaknesses, he could not be in any satisfactory sense our Way-Shower. He might be our adviser, our guide, philosopher and friend, our inspirer, our protector, our intercessor. He might have many other offices and functions, but he could not be humanity's Way-Shower unless he himself were human.

The average Christian has never discovered—indeed the fact has been carefully concealed from him—that less than any man was this Jesus a theorist and a dreamer. He has not learned that Jesus was trying to express, not the supernatural idiosyncrasies of God imperturbably dissociated from the affairs of mankind, but the views and activities of an intelligent human being struggling with the same perplexities and complexities with which other human beings struggle.

The fact which has rarely been brought home to the average Christian is that Jesus was victorious, that he emphatically made good in spite of getting in bad with the authorities to the extent of being crucified—in spite of being condemned as a menace to the established order of his time. Here again our Christian has been deceived by being theologically trained to look at Jesus, not through the eyes of his own common sense, but through the warped medium of sanctimonious emotionalism. He has been told that Jesus was poverty-stricken, despised, a failure in the sight of man, that while he was mightily rewarded after death, his human experience was one of persecution, insult, neglect, until he was left without a place to lay his head.

How warped a view this is of Jesus' life, as it is actually recorded, can be ascertained by anyone who will read the New Testament with a mind reasonably free from theological glamor and fairly capable of sensible, sane judgment.

Was Jesus desperately poor? It is hardly likely that the man who was able on at least two occasions to feed thousands by the multiplication of a few loaves of bread and a few fish ever lacked food for himself. It is hardly likely that the man who found the money for his Roman tax in a fish's mouth was without the financial means to meet all his needs. It is hardly likely that the man who sojourned with equal ease and equal honor in the home of Simon the Pharisee and that of Mary and Martha of Bethany was despised and dishonored by his fellows.

Jesus may not have had a place to lay his head in the sense of being content with material ease, comfort or routine, but he certainly was not poverty-stricken.

However humble his birth, whatever his life may have been up to the time of his public work, the end of that period found him conspicuously the most successful man of his time —indeed, the conspicuously successful man of all time. His mission, to be sure, was not understood; it still is not understood. His teachings were not comprehended; they still are not comprehended. But for unparalleled success, for making a genuine stir in the world, for gaining and keeping and thoroughly dominating the public attention, he was and is one of the most noteworthy of all examples.

It is true that he was crucified, but not because he failed. He was crucified literally because he insisted upon being crucified as the logical preliminary, according to his sense of fitness or necessity, to his most astounding success of all, his resurrection. Some may demur at accepting Jesus' resurrection as an event in his human experience. After all, if one grants other of his extraordinary achievements, some of which have been modernly duplicated—achievements which prove his freedom from many of the customary material limitations—if one admits, for instance, the possibility of raising Lazarus after three days in the tomb, there is no particular point in denying the ability of Jesus to raise himself from the dead.

In the face of the commonly held convictions regarding human limitations, the real difficulty is not the granting of Jesus' ability to return himself and others to human living after they were supposed to have passed away. Superficially accepted by the majority of Christendom as the works of a divine Person, these deeds are accounted to be evidences of the supernatural and are given no further serious consideration.

What is staggering about the resurrection of Jesus, of Lazarus, of the widow's son, of Jairus' daughter, is that they involve those who believe that they took place substantially as recorded—they involve even those who beg the question by calling them miracles—in the logical necessity of acknowledging the potential ability of other men to raise themselves and others from the dead.

"The works that I do shall he [that believeth in me] do also," [19] declared this disconcerting personage, continually insisting, not on the uniqueness of his nature and power, but on the common standing of universal humanity with him. He knew that he was no miracle worker in the sense that he was making use of a supernatural power peculiar to himself alone. He knew that he was no specially endowed individual, no exclusively chosen son of God, no exceptionally blessed of the Father.

If he said, "I and my Father are one," [20] he said it of the "I" of all men, for he also said quite as emphatically: "Why callest thou me good? There is none good but one, that is,

God." [21] Jesus' ideal of life was not an ecclesiastical hierarchy with himself at the head, but a universal brotherhood under the beneficent guidance of principle, unfolding its nature and purposes through individual right thinking and independent demonstration.

Unquestionably, like other human beings, Jesus had doubts at times, and they caused him bitter anguish. The suffering of Gethsemane was as real as any human suffering. The mental agony of the cross was genuine—far more torturing, one may surmise, than the physical pain, which he may have succeeded in overcoming by means of his understanding of mental and spiritual power.

One must remember that this man had healed multitudes of all manner of diseases. He submitted to the cross with a definite purpose in view. He told those about him that he could summon "more than twelve legions of angels" [22] if he wanted to, meaning, we may be sure, not a conquering band of heavenly personalities, but the might of Mind and Spirit to destroy all phases and forms of evil.

He had endured staggering disappointments in the repeated failures of his friends and followers—those who were particularly near to him and on whom he especially relied for understanding and help—to free themselves from the mesmerism of the traditional and grasp his point of view. He lived alone mentally and spiritually, as do all great souls. This loneliness oppressed him at times as it does others. But as a general thing, his sense of unity with the All-Knowing being keener, it must have oppressed him less than it does the usual run of mankind.

These points are made not to belittle Jesus' work or experience, but to clear away sentimental and emotional sanctimoniousness so that the true worth of his work and experience may be the better comprehended. However ecstatic the feeling may be regarding Jesus' personality, it is the custom to look upon his career on earth, measured by the standards of human accomplishment, as very much of a tragedy. There is a penetrating dramatic flavor, a gratifying theatrical appeal, in the fateful downfall of a great idealist, and this appeal is a powerful incitement to conventionalized piety. One feels so unctuously good and generous and kind when he floods his feelings with pity for the unfortunate Jesus.

Most of this emotionalism is plain cant with a fair mixture of excusable self-deception. The truth is that Jesus' career was one of the grandest successes ever achieved. He had about three years of publicity in an obscure and inconsequential Roman province. He spoke in what was even then almost a dead language. But what a name he carved for himself, what an impression he made on secular and religious history, what a world influence he became! It was an accomplishment incomparable and well-nigh incomprehensible. Anything that he said or did which will throw light on how it came about is of emphatic importance, of inestimable value to all who are endeavoring in their sphere to make a sound success of human living.

The preacher must have power. Of course, it is power for righteousness. No sane person cares for any other sort of power. Whether their power be for good or for evil, all men who have power convince themselves that it is righteous for them to have the power, even though in having it they are exceptions to all rules and all precedents. If they did not so convince themselves, they would be unable to exercise the power. Power is conviction in action.

Accomplishment signifies the possession and successful use of power. Few persons love money for itself, for the satisfaction of hoarding it. They love what the money stands for, what it brings them, what they can do with it. They love the fame of getting it. It symbolizes achievement, power.

It is because of what it signifies, rather than because of what is actually done, that makes accomplishment so tremendously important a factor in human living. The things done are quickly outgrown and forgotten. Men fancy that they build monuments, but even the pyramids hold within them the seed of disintegration. But the power that made the accomplishment possible, and the fact that someone succeeded in using the power, are eternally woven into the mental and spiritual quality of man. They are an integral part of man's immortal being.

One does not have to rely upon the *Bible*, one does not have to accept the teachings and theories of the churches, one does not have to believe matters which may be facts or may be fables, in order to know beyond question or doubt that Jesus had power—so much power that his name, if not his nature, is the one most vividly identified with our particular type of civilization.

We may not have gone as far as we might in understanding his teachings or in following his example. We may stand for long years to come, as we stood for long years gone by, on the threshold of the mighty truth that the sick can be healed and the dead can be raised by any individual man or woman who knows enough to use intelligently and consciously the everpresent forces of Mind and Spirit. But Jesus' name we have with us wherever we go, in whatever we do, with whomever we associate. As a blessing or as a curse it is on the lips of those about us many times a day every day in the year.

Whatever one may think or believe about Jesus, one cannot escape the well-nigh omnipresent evidence of Jesus' power to impress his individual quality on a vast number of men and women. They may praise him or they may damn him, but they do not ignore him and they do not forget him.

May I suggest the thought of Karl A. Menninger here when he says:

> It were better for the minister to assume that the ideals of living he preaches, the beauty of the services over which he presides with their music, their dignity, and their reflective hush, are a positive aid in the better adjustment of those who look to him, than to assume that he is more necessary to those troubled few who cannot even with these helps find happiness and health.

This does not preclude his function as a personal friend and counsellor, but it does imply that he might well draw a practical line of demarcation, as does the rest of the world, between those who are well enough to profit by his ministrations and those who are sick enough to require a doctor.

His Material—The Sermon on the Mount

The minister necessarily must know in comprehensiveness and detail the dramatic story, the literary structure, the historical context, the principles of exegesis, and the psychology of the Bible.[24]

This suggestion of Wayne E. Oates in his article, "The Diagnostic Use of the Bible" in *Pastoral Psychology* certainly is clarifying to our thought in discussing the material Jesus used in his Sermon on the Mount.

Strange as it may seem to those who have been taught to regard Jesus as the establisher of the Christian religion— stranger still to those who have been trained to look upon him as the founder and head of their particular church—the Preacher of the Sermon on the Mount was not in any degree interested in promoting a religious system. He was not concerned with the upholding of traditions, customs and conventions, sacred or otherwise.

In fact, he had evidently come to the conclusion that the moral law, so minutely prescribed by Moses and so augmented and definitized by his successors, was inadequate and faulty. The Beatitudes were perhaps intended to be more than a mere supplement to the Ten Commandments. Their purpose may have been to uncover the failure of the Ten Commandments to bring forth genuine spiritual-mindedness. Possibly they were expected to supersede the Ten Commandments.

The Preacher had learned that no code of conduct would ever discover to mankind the essential reality and being of

87

man. The preacher's passionate desire, his dominating purpose, is to introduce men and women to their true selfhood, to give them insight into spiritual values and an understanding of basic principles.

He must endeavor to convey a point of view which will make those who grasp it happier and freer, which will help them to be more successful than they have ever been in dealing with the many complexities of human living and experience. He must teach the law of life, and at the same time he must refuse to lay down rules and regulations for human beings to live by.

In the sense that he was devoted to the work of proclaiming the truth as he saw it and of making this truth clearer and of more practical worth to his fellow human beings, the Preacher was a religious teacher. But in no other sense did he touch upon religion. On the contrary, his talk was a constructive criticism, very likely in the opinion of those who listened to it a definite condemnation, of certain of the religious practices and beliefs of the times.

As an unvarnished historical fact, one will have to conclude that in the eyes of his contemporaries Jesus was a dangerous fellow, a stirrer-up of the less desirable elements in the community, a purveyor of heresies, both political and religious. He was the arch-radical of his time, and he was hated and feared by his conservative contemporaries as the radicals of all ages are invariably hated and feared by their conservative contemporaries. It is not until after the radical is safely dead that he becomes either a religious or a political prophet.

If one defines religion as the outward act or form by which men indicate their recognition of the existence of a god, then the Preacher was far from being a religious person. It is convincingly evident that outward acts, forms and ceremonials interested him not a whit.

Mankind's first religious impulses seem to have been the outgrowth of an overwhelming sense of its own inadequacies. While the Preacher may have been aware that he had much to learn, there is no indication that he had any feeling of inability to learn. It is that which the psychoanalyst calls an inferiority complex, which leads so many religiously inclined persons to find solace for their egotism and fear in imaginations about a Divine Being so big, powerful, and unrestrained that He would be quite incapable of conceiving of Himself as inadequate in relation to anything, or of being conceived of by others as inferior to anybody.

Jesus was not after this sort of comfort. He had an abiding conviction of his unity with that which he called the Father—a sense of equality and partnership with the Father. It is his sense of equality that has deceived so many into identifying him with the Father. But he did not stumble into the common human ineptitude of trying to find ways of pleasing and placating a Mighty Person, a sort of Fellow Creature of the fancy. On the contrary, Jesus was determined to show others the adequacy of themselves by proving to them the adequacy of himself.

The worship of the imaginary and unknown—homage or beseeching of the mysterious and awesome crystalized into sense-enthralling and conventionalized ceremonies—is what mankind calls religion, and being so named, is that which mankind deems sacred. In its beginnings, the worship of a Superior Being was distinctly materialistic and selfish. It was begotten by the animal instinct for self-preservation. Today, even in its most spiritualized development and expression, the materialistic taint still clings.

Habits of judgment—the way the mind more or less unconsciously reacts to certain conditions and situations—are more keenly indicative of states of mind than are verbal claims and theoretical beliefs. Those who judge by appearances, by conventions, by conformities, do so because appearances are to them basically important, because conventions are to them inherently righteous, because they believe that the finer qualities of mind and spirit can be gained and kept by promoting prescribed details of outward conduct.

The Preacher of the Sermon on the Mount was not so

deluded. He was not devoted to any person or group of persons. He had no theory of salvation nor any way of salvation by means of outward forms or inward beliefs. He outlined no system of church government, not even a code of human conduct. However much these things and other things like them might absorb the attention, arouse the ardor and stimulate the self-sacrifice of others, they were not of deep-seated importance to him. He did not preach the Sermon on the Mount to set any of them forth or to uphold any of them.

The Sermon on the Mount is an inspirationally conceived appeal to reason. It is what Dr. Weigle is saying when he states: "We are impressed with the reasonableness as well as with the directness of Jesus' appeal to those who heard him." [25] Further, Dean Weigle tells us: "Thus the Sermon on the Mount becomes the incontestable charter of liberal Christianity." [26] It is logical argument spiritually illuminated. The purpose of Jesus was first to awaken his hearers to the tremendous necessity of thinking for themselves, and then to give them something fundamentally conclusive to think about. He was motived by an ardent, self-absorbing devotion to the truth. He manifested this devotion not by conformity to established beliefs and dominant activities, but by his own free individual thinking, by actions which were the intelligent evidence of his free individual thinking, and furthermore, by encouraging his listeners to think and act with equal conviction and independence. He was doing what George Coe states in *What Is Christian Education?* regarding preaching:

What is recognized as the greatest preaching of today does not endeavor to do people's thinking for them, but to awaken thinking on their part. It does not impose cut-and-dried duties upon them, but makes them sensitive toward ethical actualities, and then relies upon them to find their duties.[27]

When the words of the Preacher are removed from the theological cloud of a sham solemnity, when they are read as the words of a man and not piously and perfunctorily as those of a far-away God-Person, they flame with purpose and power. When the words of Jesus were first uttered, they were flung straight into the face of the self-satisfied and hypocritical. They are today a fiery rebuke to those who would find merit through abiding by the letter of the law. They call today as they did at first for individual conviction. Heeded, they uproot the platitudinous. They destroy mass mesmerism. They make thinkers who reach for principles before they commit themselves to systems.

Jesus had a reason for both his sayings and his doings. He knew that human ignorance is not the road to divine understanding, but he also knew that the attainment of human knowledge is not a worthwhile end in itself. Therefore, those who profit by the words of Jesus are bound to learn for themselves and from their experiences that there is no final satisfaction in a theory about the truth. They are bound to learn that in order to really know anything, they must discern it through individual realization, understand it through individual thinking, and finally through individual living prove that they understand it.

The paramount effectiveness of the Sermon on the Mount is not because it is a guide to religious life, for the Preacher was not primarily a religious man. It is not because it is a help to a more harmonious communal living, for the Preacher was not an especially good citizen. It is not because it answers the bewildered cry of the human heart, *What shall I do to be saved?* The Preacher had no counsel acceptable to those who sought a mechanical means of salvation assuring to their irresponsibility. He knew that the cry could not be answered in terms of doing.

Superbly distinguished from the entire horde of reformers, the Preacher did not instruct his hearers either how to do good or how not to do evil. His sublime originality was in putting before all men, regardless of their peculiar religious, racial or personal beliefs, what they must *be* in order to be themselves. He told them the qualities of mind and spirit they

91

must have, how they must feel, in order to be the men that they really are. Instead of a way to be saved, he set forth unmistakably and emphatically what a man is when he is saved.

The iridescence of a living, eternal truth shone through the simple words simply spoken by Jesus, "Except ye become as little children." [28] Unburdened by tradition, untrammeled by conventions, free to feel, spontaneous to express, impulsive, natural, emotionally unashamed, receptive to the new, curious about the unknown, questioning, willing to learn—such are they who did find, and who now can find, the iridescence of a living, eternal truth in the Sermon on the Mount.

Conversion

The stages of the process of conversion are just those found in working out any intense problem under pressure—first, a sense of perplexity and uneasiness; second, a climax and turning point; and third, a relaxation marked by rest and joy.[29]

Thus Dr. Ames clearly defines the problem of conversion. Further, he very frankly states his conviction that

Unless conversion is preceded or followed by the effective development of habits belonging to good character, then conversion becomes a momentary emotion with no positive significance.[30]

"Brother, are you saved?" Many times this question is thrust into the vision and hearing of each of us. It generally arouses one of two emotions, one of resentment or one of curiosity. We resent it because we are irked that anyone should feel we are so stupid as to be solicited in such a pointed manner. Or our curiosity is aroused because we wonder what is the drive that forces people to ask such questions.

Webster notes conversion in theology as "the change of belief and life, either immediate or gradual, manifested by one forsaking unbelief, either active or apathetic, to take up the worship of God; change of heart." [31]

What we are concerned with here is the *immediate* or *gradual* part of the change.

Let us look at the one of *immediate* change. This is usually an emotional experience, the result of apparent frustration on the part of the individual. On the one hand all life has come down to one focal point. The individual through his experiences has come to an end of all effort. Frustration manifests itself on every hand. What can be done? Nothing except give up and in that very giving up the individual is afforded an escape from frustration. This escape may come in one of two ways. Suicide or the recovery of balance in reality through the catharsis and therapy of religious values.

On the other hand the group in which the individual moves may be one that encourages this immediate response through group hypnotism induced by suggestion, etc. The most common of these experiences is the revival meeting. Plans are laid well in advance of the meeting and through publicity and personal work a fever of excitement is built up culminating in the actual week or month of meetings. Many writers have gone into detail describing these experiences of both a group nature and the response of the individual within these groups. It has become quite clear that too many times the emotions are not backed up with the necessary intellectual thought. It has the tendency to create hypocrites rather than Christians. Afterthought sometimes results in resentment, as with other emotional responses, and the individual is really a loss to religion rather than a gain. There has not been a true catharsis and therapy.

Regardless of how this *immediate* change comes there are those who argue for it and those who argue against it. However, it should be judged in the light of end results.

Let us look at the *gradual* change idea of conversion.

Here we can see that education must play a large part. We evolve, as it were, to higher and higher stages of understanding of religious values until there is a crystalization of thinking which may or may not result in conversion. For instance, this growth may come to be in this manner. The individual may learn more and more about religion until he becomes fixed in his growth, stereotyped, as it were, and failing to be really converted to its ways he becomes one who merely gives lip service to it. Here again we see there are dangers and arguments for and against this method. Again its true therapy can only be truthfully judged in the measure of end achievements.

Undoubtedly there are those who must travel different routes to the attainment of this conversion experience if they are to get it at all. For we know people are different according to both heredity and environment. Also we know intelligence is not restricted to a particular group, race, or faith. Therefore, when we set aside our personal prejudices and look at both the *immediate* change and the *gradual* one, asking ourselves and statistics which is advantageous, we may arrive at the answer.

The lasting effects for the therapy of conversion are weighed heavily in favor of the *gradual* one. Statistics show that 75% of conversions come in adolescence. This is because of the educational approach. Do not, however, be misled by this. Conversion is not the end result. This is an action, yes, but is it a continual one? If the educational program is one that continues and does not stop relating action to thinking, then it will be most effective. But the paradox is that this does not always happen and, also that those who are converted with an *immediate* experience in many instances bring forth fruits more worthy of acceptance.

Is it not possible then that both methods have something to be said for them? Is it not possible that applying the catharsis and therapy of the personal and individual touch as Jesus did with his disciples is a better way? A way that will, in end results, prove lasting and enduring? We all have many different experiences and it is difficult for us to appreciate another's viewpoint, for we react to our experiences in multiple ways.

In my summary here, which is an attempt at showing the relation of conversion to therapeutic preaching, may I make these observations:

1. Preaching in order to heal effectively must afford to the individual the means whereby he can arrive at this experience successfully regardless of whether the change is *immediate* or *gradual*.

2. Preaching in order to heal effectively must make the individual's problems its problems.

3. Preaching in order to heal effectively must be concerned with verbs, not adjectives.

The results of this over-all vision and action in the drama of preaching will be:

1. A spiritual regeneration that will weld together Christendom's warring dissensions into a mighty healing force for good.

2. An environment will be created that will permit the discovery of much we do not know now about God and our relations to him.

3. Therapeutic religion will come into being. For religion is not religion at all unless it heals, and one of these therapies is that of conversion. Is it not?

Let us come back to our earlier question, "Brother, are you saved?" These individuals who irk us or arouse our curiosity are the victims of an imposed group pattern which feels certain reactions and responses must be experienced by the individual or he is not saved. These people need help and need it badly. They are not to be ignored and snubbed, but rather helped. Intellectual snobbery is not the answer. Preaching must heal here in this fringe field or it will miss its greatest opportunity. Uncontrolled fanaticism can swamp us all. It almost did in the recent war. It may next time. This "Brother are you saved?" question must be answered, for it rears its head in many places and in numerous fashions. The therapeutic value inherent in the drama of preaching is one of the answers.

The Sacraments

This topic deals with the two sacraments held by Protestants to be such, Baptism and Communion. Hiltner is illustrative here when he states:

> The sacraments and rites of the Church are not intended to have anything inherent taken away from them by considering the way in which the pastor may utilize them in connection with counseling. The point is rather that we have in all Protestant churches particular acts which may have a meaning deeper than words—not only because of their age but also because they symbolize the relation between fundamental religious truth and the most common acts of life. Baptism is not only ancient; it also symbolizes rebirth in its linkage of earth's most common fluid with spiritual regeneration. The communion links the commonest of man's daily acts, eating and drinking, with the most sublime fellowship.[32]

Preface

Goal. If we can create in the mind of the participant an awe, a reverence, a love for fellowship with both God and his fellow men in the experience of these sacraments held to be of such great worth to the Protestant faith, we will be successful in our purpose.

All inclusive participation. If the impression of a true catharsis on the mind, heart, and soul is accomplished, then not alone are we creating the correct atmosphere for therapy, thus helping the participant, but we are bringing into focus the lives of those not yet so doing, those who up to this witnessing have been solely spectators.

Concerted action. Then not alone do we receive the participant, but the spectator as well. For a return to the experience by the participant and a participation by the spectator will bring into being a unity of thought resulting in action. For to insure the bonds of fellowship in Christian brotherhood we have to knit the spiritual lives of people together.

Ethical ideal. We are attempting to deal with the return *to the familiar* both by the participant and the spectator. This should challenge us to make the original experience, the *to be familiar*, a satisfying, desirable, joyous, intensely dramatic religious impression.

The familiar. The use of the drama of Holy Communion, the keeping of Christ at the center of life and living should so become a part of the life of the individual that its use will always be turned to when decisions must be made and when the stresses of life become heavy and overbearing.

Transfer of experience of the familiar, possible and logical. Why? How? The limit of time in the average church worship program today does not always permit the proper emphasis to be made dramatically upon the worshiper. Therefore, in order to better captivate the emotions, the best setting sometimes for the service in question, communion, should be a separate one away from the regular morning worship program. For as Gladden tells us:

> They are symbols of spiritual facts and relations,— beautiful symbols which may greatly aid in impressing upon our minds these spiritual facts and in leading us to enter joyfully into these spiritual relations.
>
> The history of Baptism, beginning with the Day of Pentecost and coming down through the first five centuries of the life of the Church is a striking illustration of the growth of ritualistic elements.[33]

Further he summarizes his thought and ours when he says:

> There is a theory here of the nature of baptism which is still held in a large part of Christendom. It supposes a transaction of great and vital importance; it connotes a belief that in the performance of the rite a spiritual change is wrought upon the recipient. The phraseology of some of the Protestant rituals expresses this belief, and the rite of Exorcism, which is part of the baptismal service, not only in the Roman Catholic Church, but in some branches of the Lutheran church, possesses a significance which cannot be ignored.[34]

We realize this statement places us in a position which is wide open to criticism, but permit us to carry through to the end. *Thus it is possible to afford a transfer of experience from a special service to regular services, making the transition to the shorter regular one richer and fuller of meaning.* Isn't it important to serve *meaning* as well as *time*, especially in regard to matters eternal? For example, the Episcopal Church, which successfully helps utilize the medium of dramatic pageantry, affords a special service for baptism and communion aside from the regular worship service. The communion service is offered every Lord's Day. In addition, they make possible communion services throughout the week from one Lord's Day to another. Coe asks a question here and gives us the answer:

> What, then, of Christian education that centres in the worship of the church, and that seeks to make of this worship a mental living over, and thereby a spiritual appropriation, of the divine drama enacted in the life, death, and resurrection of Jesus? The focal points in such education are two: Instruction in the Scriptural origins of the church, its history, and its

constitution and usages, and participation in the worship and the life of the church. In one of its forms, this theory makes the sacraments the channels through which God's saving grace flows, and then education is directed toward feelingful and habitual participation therein, particularly in the eucharist. Increasing voluntary frequency at the communion is then taken as one of the surest signs of religious growth.[35]

Now it is not thought impossible to effectively conduct a regular morning worship service containing both baptism and communion, presenting them dramatically. However, the average church does not have a rich enough background of dramatic pageantry to realize and appreciate the values inherent in these sacraments. As Gladden suggests: "To append the Communion to a service of ordinary length is not wise." [36] What is right for one sacrament should be right for another.

Can we not assume that these special services will be basically for the purpose of indirect and unconscious education in the beauty and loveliness of properly worshiping God? Isn't the ministry a teaching one? Isn't it time incoming members were prepared with something more than the simple statement now presented to them when they come forward? Isn't the pastor responsible to God for planting a little more seed than he does or possibly can in the few minutes he is *allowed to preach on Sunday mornings?* To insure the bonds of fellowship in Christian brotherhood we have to tie people together spiritually. In order for people to work together groupwise they have to know each other. When this is accomplished, if ever, people become community-minded, that is, they know how to work together churchwise and churchwide. They become CHURCHMEN in the best sense.

Hence, pastor's classes should be conducted resulting in special services, our topic here and now. *Result:* An educated laity building the Kingdom of God in their lives and the lives of others, not alone in the worship services of the church—

these are understood to be the peak of religious experience—but in the everyday relationships of their lives one with another. If we are of Christ we should reflect Christ!

Dr. Robinson encourages us in our thinking where he explains in *The Biblical Doctrine of the Church:*

This new society had its own rite of initiation—baptism in the name of Jesus Christ—and its own fellowship worship—"the breaking of bread and the prayers"—as well as its own daily school of instruction after the manner of the synagogue (Acts 2:42).[37]

Further he speaks in reference to Paul's thought of the church as the body of Christ:

Certainly in all that he writes, his mind is influenced by the close relationship between the sacraments of baptism and the Lord's Supper, on the one hand, and the church or the body of Christ, on the other hand, and the relationship of each Christian, who is a member of the church, to the Incarnate Christ and to the Spirit whom he sends.[38]

The Sacrament of Baptism

One of the most treasured experiences in the work of the Master is that of the baptismal service. In this ritual, which is a law to be kept, but at the same time an experience to be felt, if there is to be a catharsis and a therapy, no pastor should miss the golden opportunity that is his, when conducting this service, to make it so valuable an experience that the new disciple will remember it regularly for the rest of his or her life, particularly when the storms of life beset them.

Preparation for Baptism. In preparing the candidates for baptism it is good to guide their thinking in the proper direction. Make their thoughts Christ-centered. This can be done effectively with the proper use of music, direct participation on their part and on the part of the congregation. Always choose the great hymns of the church in the service. The ones that have lasting qualities and whose meanings are sacred and Christ-centered are important. Place these through the service with the thought in mind of building towards a climax. Prepare a suitable pledge to their call of the church for the candidates. Follow that with a hymn of consecration, then use a dedication of the candidates with the congregation participating. Conclude it with a fitting confession of beliefs for the candidates using scripture passages. A hymn guiding them to the pool for baptism would help the service here.

Actual Baptism. The candidate, or candidates, are prepared for the climax and have successfully arrived at the point where the actual ceremony takes place. Conduct this part of the service with the greatest of care, for here is where true catharsis and therapy are created. The candidate has been looking forward to this moment with great anticipation or with great fear. It is well known how some people have a great fear of being submerged completely in water. A person of this temperament should be handled with the utmost consideration. If you have more than one in a family have them come into the pool together. This will in many cases give courage to the others in the family being baptized, if they are in a group. Here is a suggestion that can be, and has been, used effectively. Have someone, preferably the church school superintendent or an elder, read a passage of scripture pertaining to baptism, such as: Matt. 3:13-17, Mark 1:9-11, Rom. 6:1-11, immediately before you baptize the candidates. This definitely ties the candidate to New Testament teachings. Following this dramatic climax in the service have the congregation sing appropriate hymns and use a prayer to fit the occasion while the candidates and you are getting dressed.

Procession to the New Life. Here is the placing of the bow upon the knot you have tied in conducting the actual baptism. This is a part that definitely ties the candidate to actual participation in church worship. Let us not forget that having secured confessions from many people and having baptized these same ones it is wrong to let them feel that salvation is completed in the baptismal service by the failure to tie them up with the sacrament of the church we hold so dear, the Lord's Supper. Let us suggest that the actual baptismal service be followed with the procession to the new life. Let the pastor, carrying the Bible—the Word of God—open, lead the procession from the back of the church to the altar, followed by the elders bearing the Cross, to represent that through Christ we have a living faith. Let the deacons follow bearing the symbols of the sacrifice on the Cross for all men and, following the deacons, the candidates each bearing a lighted candle telling that Christ is the Light of the World.

Then afford a period of silence concluding it with the candidates making the following suggested resolutions for the Lord's Supper:

I will never jest or make fun of those whom others condemn.

I will never allow myself to hate any living man or woman.

I will strive to keep my heart free and brave that I may live like Jesus in all things.

I will, at the Lord's Table, shut out the world, the noise, and be silent before the Lord.

I will fix my heart on my Master, therefore I cannot be cold to my brother.

First Communion. The communion hymn can be followed here by the elders and deacons serving the new members of their flock the Lord's Supper. After the communion service another climax has been reached and it is wise to have the candidates pledge something like this:

Deep in my heart I know that the church is of God. That she has made my community and my country a better place in which to live, to work, and to establish my home. That I would not want to live or die in a land where no church spires point its people heavenward. In this knowledge I gladly give myself to my church and offer her my loyal support by intelligent membership, regular attendance, generous giving, ardent prayer, and devoted service.

In order to complete this service effectively it is good to present the new members of the church with appropriate baptismal certificates. Then close with a hymn and the benediction.

The suggestions above have been found to have therapeutic value for the baptismal service. Think about these things: Preparation for Baptism; Actual Baptism; Procession to the New Life; The First Communion.[39]

The Sacrament of Communion

Analysis of a Communion Service held New Year's Eve, December 31, 1949, in the Old Stone Church, East Haven, Connecticut.

This was an attempt to accomplish what J. S. Whale states in his book, *Christian Doctrine:* "Thus, in the full diet of public worship in every church throughout Christendom, two permanent elements together constitute 'the means of grace' "; [40] and he notes as the "second, the Sacrament of the Eucharist, where the highest is not spoken but acted; where the promises of the gospel are visibly sealed by the Yea and Amen of a ritual act." [41] Earlier in his work Whale quotes Calvin in what has a direct meaning to the therapeutic value in the sacrament of communion, thus: " 'Let us understand,' says Calvin, 'that this sacrament is a medicine for the poor spiritual sick.' " [42]

A spirit of fellowship was created before this service with participation in an hour of games and singing. At eleven-thirty all were asked to assemble quietly in the sanctuary which had been prepared for the service of communion.

During the assembling of the participants the organist created an atmosphere of solemn quiet through the organ prelude. This was the initial step in encouraging humility in the act of appreciation. To create in the mind's eye of those

103

who attended a vision of God was the endeavor. To encourage this feeling a large white candle had been placed on a pedestal directly behind the cross in the center of the lower level of the worship center. It was the only candle lighted before the service started. Directly in front of the cross was a piece of plastiglass on which was etched an 8 x 10 picture of Christ, "Thy Kingdom Come," by Signe E. Larson, 1933. This was mounted on a mahogany base, which afforded light from within the glass to display the picture.

Hence the real worship center was a picture of Christ backed up by the cross which in turn was overshadowed with light, candlelight, symbolic of Jesus Christ, and this in turn of God our Father and His Father.

The illumination in the church was as subdued as was possible and still enable those attending light enough to follow the program.

Immediately after all were assembled fourteen candles, seven on each side of the large white candle, were lighted, bearing testimony of the seven deacons who were originally called in the early church to minister to the need of the church. Here they represent the followers of Jesus.

After this all joined in the singing of "Sweet Hour of Prayer." Here the mood of *humility* was stressed through music. That music was familiar. Following this the scripture was read directing the feeling of *humility* towards light. In this setting the emphasis was *appreciation*, *contemplation*, and an *interpretation* through symbols seen, participated in, and heard, leading to *capitulation*. These were all utilized to create the proper initial environment.

Then, through singing by the entire group of a hymn of *dedication*, the vitality of the moment was captured. A *measure of judgment* was passed by those sharing this experience, directing somewhat of a *change of vision*.

The lighting of the candles was now performed to symbolize the characteristics Jesus made manifest here on earth. A poetic commentary on candles prefaced this part of the service. Following this the young people selected for the purpose came forward and lighted colored candles in the candelabra on each side of the worship center. Each young person carried a small candle which was used to carry the light from the large white candle at the worship center to the colored candle. As each young person lighted a different colored candle the appropriate phrase explaining the emblematic implication of the color was given by the leader of the service. Here we find *recollection* being encouraged through *apprecition, contemplation,* and *interpretation.*

Following the lighting of the colored candles by the young people, during which the organist had played "Follow The Gleam," the leader of the service called the twelve disciples by name as they are noted in the New Testament. As each name was called a layman would come forward carrying a tall white candle which was lighted from the large white candle at the worship center. Then each one would go up to the altar and place the white candle in a holder provided for that purpose on the Lord's Table. When all were assembled around the table they were seated. The entire assemblage then joined in the singing of "Here at Thy Table, Lord."

Here were assembled men holding the light cast by the disciples of that far-off day when Jesus observed the Passover with them in the Upper Room. Here were emblematic lights directing the thoughts of those attending to God. This mood of *humility* was encouraged through appropriate background music by the organist. Here was light used to illuminate the hearts, minds, and souls of the people with God.

The service from this point was by candlelight. Now followed the order of worship for the taking of communion, the leader giving it to the disciples and they in turn giving it to the worshipers. The solidarity of the group was reflected in the taking of the bread together at the signal of the pastor and in like manner the taking of the cup together. It should be noted that the service was so timed that the observers of

105

the sacrament were holding their cups when the hour of midnight came. The church bell was rung for about one minute at the stroke of twelve.

In all of this it can be seen the forms are simple and their meanings stressed. The environment for all of this was in keeping with a sense of *humble* worship. *Solidarity* was emphasized through the joint participation of those assembled in the acts of observance.

Dedication to finer living in a *humble* walk with God was now pointed to with the singing of the New Year's Hymn. A change of vision for those at this service was hoped and prayed for and in a measure realized. From *personal testimonies* following the service we are confident this is true. From *later action* meriting such testimony we are convinced of its *therapeutic value.*

After the sanctuary was empty of worshipers the candles, except the large white one at the worship center, were extinguished by the leader of the service. Announcement had been made beforehand that there would be an observance of a twenty-four-hour vigil of prayer following this communion service. The pastor was the first on the list for this vigil and then followed laymen and laywomen.

It was an experience this old historic church had never had before. It is hoped it will benefit thereby. During that twenty-four hours there were two other formal church services at which communion was observed as it had been at midnight. Personal testimony and action since have proven the worth of this—in a sense—departure from the stereotype form of communion. It can be said that this dramatization of the Upper Room experience of long ago, when properly done, can move people so they come to know the therapeutic values in the peace that comes from God, our Maker.

Prayer

Under the question of "What is Worship?" [43] James Black, in *The Mystery of Preaching*, states, "Worship is the

106

church on its knees." [44] This being true, we must consider the therapy of prayer and ask ourselves questions regarding it.

Kirby Page, in *Living Prayerfully*, feels:

Every element in prayer is needed to produce the most exalted symphony of life. By nature man is a praying creature endowed with inexhaustible powers of response to God's loving and persistent appeal to climb to high levels of communion and fellowship.[45]

Let us look at some different facets of prayer through the eye of interrogation.

How is Prayer to be distinguished, if at all, from Autosuggestion?

Prayer and autosuggestion have a definite relationship. That relationship is one of advancement. Autosuggestion can and should be the place where our thinking is aroused to become interested in a need. That felt need is, in this instance, prayer. Of course, there are those who feel that this is self-hypnotism and should be guarded against. However, these same folks never do much of anything for themselves or others, for they are so afraid of everything about which they don't know. They have lost the spirit of adventure, the spirit of pioneering, if you will. Therefore, autosuggestion, to my thinking, is a tool, a method, whereby we can encourage ourselves to *be*. It is a means, not an end. Even prayer is not an end in itself. It too is a furtherance of self-expression, to a fulfillment through growth. To not grow is to sin. Hence, we can see that prayer, growth, and sin are related. Lack of prayer retards growth and sin becomes the rider in the saddle of unfulfilled desire and need. Dr. Buttrick writes, "The integration wrought by prayer goes far beyond health of body and 'mind'—as it must be convincing, for all men must die: prayer grants wholeness of vision and motive." [46]

How is Prayer to be distinguished, if at all, from Interhuman Communication?

Prayer and interhuman communication have a definite relationship. Not as prayer and autosuggestion have they a relationship, but in a different sense. We do not know the fulfillment of mental telepathy yet. Here we are thinking of what we now know. If our prayers are purely self-centered they cannot be truly prayers. They must have a relationship to others. This must be because of two reasons. Both of these reasons fail to take into account the higher reason that God requires it. These reasons are: Because of what happens to other people; and because of what happens to us. Other people are moved more by what happens to us than what happens to themselves. This facet of interhuman communication has not been too well understood.

Autosuggestion leads to prayer, and prayer without the feeling of interhuman communication is futile. If we see our neighbor practicing golf and making a good score we seek to follow his pattern. But if we see him practicing without the attendant results we become skeptical. It is at this point where the higher reason enters the picture: the reason that God requires of man certain functions. We may practice intercessory prayer without apparent results. This should not cause us to become discouraged in our efforts. For the problem may not be our neighbor or God, but ourselves. Therefore to practice in prayer interhuman communication as well as human-God communication will be discouraging, but those who press on to the ever-receding goal will find the Christlike reflections of their own actions bearing far greater weight in the balance than they ever realized. Important to us here are the words of encouragement voiced by Bushnell in *Christian Nurture:*

To the manner in which prayers, of all kinds, get their answer from God. Two things are wanted, as conditions previous to the favoring answer. First, that

the matter requested should agree with God's beneficent aims, or the ends of good to which his plans are
built. Secondly, that the prayer should agree with as
many other prayers, and as many other circles of
causes as possible; for God is working always toward
the largest harmony, and will not favor, therefore,
the prayers of words, when everything else in the life
is demanding something else, but will rather have
respect to what has the widest reach of things and persons making suit with it.[47]

What is the Relationship of Prayer to Belief?

Prayer has a definite relationship to belief. Here we are
passing over into achievements rather than dealing with
initiatives as we have up to this point. While belief is not
enough in itself to be called an achievement, in the strict
sense, it is certainly a step towards the goal of knowing God.
We have beliefs in many things today. Few of us ever sort
them out and classify them according to their proper valua-
tion. It is often said that people have too many beliefs and not
enough convictions. A belief is the hypothesis upon which
the scientist builds his experiment. In *Jesus Came Preaching*,
Buttrick explains:

In that secret quest called prayer! Science is noble,
but science also derives her strength from hidden wells
whose life-giving stream flows clear in One we call the
Christ.[48]

Therefore we find belief being the basis upon which the one
who prays places his autosuggestion, and the encouragement
of that autosuggestion is made through interhuman communication as well as human-God communication, the result being
an established belief. Hence it is seen that belief is both a
part of the initial thinking and effort as well as the achievement of that same thinking and effort.

What is the Relationship of Prayer to Faith?

Prayer is the food upon which faith feeds. If there is one single word of fact that ties together all the thinking of the Old and New Testament it is faith. Further if there is one single word of fact that makes faith the strong motif it is, that word is prayer. All the great religious faiths known to man found their succor in the establishment of periods of solitude where through contemplation, prayer, men came to realize their responsibility to a higher power, or good—could it be God?—and to their fellow men, the result being faith. If man would have strong faith he must feed what he has with strong prayer. Dr. Buttrick illustrates this:

> If the New Testament account of the temptation of Jesus is His dramatization of a desperate inner testing (a testing the more desperate because He hungered only for the coming of the Kingdom of God), must we not recognize that there Jesus confronted the alternative of a social crusade on the one hand and, on the other, the revealing of God?—and that His victory, though at cost of a Cross, was in choosing to be the revealer of God rather than the leader of a national or economic crusade? "Social service" must remain a truncated endeavor, ever drained by the ebbing of its zeal, until it makes terms with the fact that Jesus (the one Benefactor) spent whole nights in prayer.[49]

What is the Relationship of Prayer to Action?

Action is the result of prayer. Through prayer man comes to know what his action should be. Christ certainly delineated that in his seeking of his father in the period of temptation following his baptism. Time and time again he resorted to periods of solitude, prayer, when he sought to know the will of his Father. At the early age of twelve, when he was found by his parents in the temple, he explained that he must be about his Father's business. Always through prayer Christ came to know what his line of action was to be, and knowing that he pressed on with courageous heart and bold endeavor to follow it. Again Buttrick affords us light in the statement:

Our record of Him is so fragmentary that not more than one hundred days (perhaps not more than sixty days) have any mention. Yet we read repeatedly that He went into a mountain to pray. Three times we are told that He spent half the night in prayer. He prayed at His Baptism, at the tidings of the death of John the Baptist, at the coming of those Greeks who seemed to Him the first fruits of a world-wide harvest, at the Last Supper, in the Garden of Gethsemane—and on the Cross. At every crisis of joy or sorrow, at every onset of new responsibility, at every crucial decision, at the sounding of every new challenge—He prayed.[50]

If the interpretations given above are practiced, beliefs will become convictions and from those convictions Christian faith will motivate resultant Christian action. For we are in agreement with Dr. Buttrick that the greatest argument in favor of prayer is to pray.[51] He, Dr. Buttrick, closes his book on *Prayer* with a vivid picture:

A certain pastor, who lives where simple faith is shadowed by dark persecution, was asked to tell the secret of his calm endurance. "When the house is dark," he answered, "I do not try to sweep away darkness with a broom: I light a candle." Prayer is more than a lighted candle: it is the contagion of health. It is the pulse of Life.[52]

In closing this thought we illustrate the drama of prayer in a quotation from Eugene L. Smith in *Pastoral Psychology:*

111

The spiritual climax of the wedding, however, comes immediately after that. For the first thing you do as husband and wife is to kneel together. No symbolism could be more appropriate. The first thing that you say in your married life is The Lord's Prayer. I never cease to marvel at the meaning of that Prayer in that moment. This is your first action in that new life. No action could do more of itself to make the two of you really one than to say together this prayer with full devotion to its deepest meaning.[53]

Yes, there are therapeutic values in prayer.

Music

Introduction

Physicians throughout the world are beginning to realize that music is of definite value in keeping the mind and body healthy. Those in the field of insanity in particular have long known that music is one of the best medicines for the mind. Many feel so keenly about it they think that if every hospital or asylum inducted a musical director into its medical staff, or if every physician and trained musician understood the nature and action of music, untold good might be accomplished, with lives brightened and tangled brains restored to harmony.

Dr. Luther E. Woodward, in his article, "Contributions of the Minister to Mental Hygiene," states our case in these words:

The very persistence of the custom of worship suggests that there is mental hygiene value in it, although worship programs have not usually been devised with this in mind. They have been built up on the basis of a particular theology or the liturgical usage of some historic period rather than on psychological laws and principles. They are effective, of course, to the degree that they observe psychological laws (devisedly or accidentally) and fit the particular emotional needs of the worshippers. If the worship meets their feeling needs and leaves them less in conflict and more secure, they hold to it. If it offends them less in conflict and more secure, they hold to it. If it offends their aesthetic taste or intellectual integrity or if it moves in a system of thought and feeling that is unfamiliar, people naturally turn away from it, for they find in it no real value for themselves.[54]

Music has definite, measurable effects on the body and mind. It has, as exhaustive tests have proved, a direct effect on the pulse, respiration and blood pressure, these accelerating or retarding, rising or lowering, in response to different rhythms. It has also, an effect on the ductless glands, thus influencing the emotions. Music harmonizes conflicting moods which depress the nervous system. This leads us to accept as factual the statements of Dr. Clifton E. Kew and the Reverend Clinton J. Kew in their article, "Group Psychotherapy In a Church Setting," regarding the value of music as a part of group therapy in the church. We quote:

> Group therapy is as old as human history: human beings seem always to have formed therapeutic groups to gain relief and support from their fellow men. Even in the mysterious hieroglyphics of the ancient writings we find references to the groups as a means of emotional support and spiritual uplift. Therapy has taken many forms—as music, drama, lecture, play, dancing, and so forth. However, its most notable form has been religious. Moses, Jesus, and St. Paul all used the restorative forces of group interaction to bring relief and support to their congregations through singing, prayers, sermons, and versicles.[55]

The Romanists, with their emphasis upon ritual, defend their position and afford a splendid argument for the conduct of their services in the work of Dr. Charles Dreisoerner in *The Psychology of Liturgical Music*, specifically in the "Epilogue," where he speaks of the assistance afforded by liturgical music to the integration of self:

> Religion offers psychologically one of the most important factors in this work of integration, precisely because it allows by its very nature a synthesis of the physical and the human in the divine. In religion, liturgical services with all their implications of community spirit and divine institution offer psychologically an ideal framework for this religious synthesis to develop. And in this framework, music—that marvelous synthesis of the physical and the spiritual—appears as a most useful instrument, if only man will take care to use it with ear fixed upon what is religious in it, with his mind set upon the divine things of which its text speaks to him, and with his heart raised to God with all the warmth of sentiment of which music has the secret.[56]

Influences

The *power of music* to act as therapy rests upon the close affinity between the human organism and rhythm, as well as the capacity of the human mind to respond to it by mental symbols. Recent work in this field has proved that music rhythm has a profound effect on brain rhythm, and thus on brain function. In understanding that the mechanics of the human brain can be affected by music sounds, physicians have applied this knowledge as a means of *healing* by reaching into the innermost mental and emotional life of listeners.

Music therapy, begun in our mental hospitals some years back, is presently a recognized method of treatment, applied to thousands of patients suffering from various types of mental disturbance such as delusions, hallucinations, fears and depressions. They receive music in the wards for regular periods during the week. Especially selected music is played for the different wards: for the violent patients soothing music is played; for the depressed and lethargic, lively, stimulating music is prescribed. No matter what the condition, when music is played it has been observed that patients, as well as normally healthy men and women, react to it by tapping their feet, drumming their fingers or swaying their bodies in time with the rhythm, thus indicating that the music has succeeded in capturing their attention.

Effectiveness

In a study of *music therapy* for patients at the state hospital at Eloise, Michigan, Dr. Ira M. Altshuler found that soft music was an ideal therapy for general use, 35 per cent more effective than the wet sheet pack which is used routinely in quieting insane patients. Dr. Altshuler enumerates the following chief attributes of music for mental patients:

1. Capacity to produce changes in metabolism, respiration, blood pressure, pulse and endocrine and muscular energy.
2. Ability to command attention and increase its span.
3. Power of diversion and substitution (as distracting patients from morbid states and replacing with wholesome feelings and ideas).
4. Capacity to modify the mood.
5. Capacity to stimulate pictorially and intellectually.[57]

Working with these established facts, doctors, nurses, or anyone caring for an invalid, a convalescent, or a victim of mental disorder can put music to practical use as a means for greater healing and happiness. In addition to the valuable work music is doing in the hospitals, asylums and prisons, it is also of great value in industrial life. In shops and factories it is being used more and more to relieve the tedium of monotonous tasks. It speeds up work and affords relief from the din, as well as combating fatigue and increasing employee efficiency.

Usage

Today, with the radio, television and perfected phonograph, we can have the wholesome benefits of music in our homes, almost when we will, at very little cost. Music should become as much of a daily factor in building and maintaining health as proper diet and sleep.

These suggestions and experiments pointing to the therapeutic values inherent in music both for the secular and the religious aspects of life leads us to agree with Joseph Ashton when he says:

> It is not by mere accident that music has always been used in religious worship, for religion and music arise from the same general part of our being. Religion is the most intimate of all human experiences, and music is the most intimate of the arts. Music is at once the most subjective, and the least concrete of all the arts; its subjectiveness is the most personal, its substance the least tangible. It has the very valuable property of stimulating the emotions and strengthening consciousness, yet at the same time regulating them through the sense of balance and proportion inherent in the art of music itself. Music is thus the ideal art for religious worship.[58]

Alfred B. Haas points out:

> One of the most important areas of help in breaking down the feeling of loneliness and despair ex-

perienced by so many today is in the field of hymns. The hymn gathers the faithful together round the treasure of life which it contains, and breaks down as nothing else can the isolation of the soul. Because of the rich and deep emotional associations which music supplies, and because these associations are even more far-reaching when familiar words become bound up with the tunes, a hymn used in *corporate worship*, by choir and congregation, may:

(1) Focus attention outside of preoccupation with self,
(2) bring comfort,
(3) reduce anxiety,
(4) alleviate the sense of guilt, and
(5) strengthen inner resolves [59]

He concludes:

What we would urge to those in the pastoral ministry is to explore this field of the therapeutic value of hymns, for Sunday after Sunday, persons are either helped, or hindered, by the wise, or careless, choice of the hymns used in *corporate worship*.[60]

The power of music to influence the mind and affect the emotions has long been known. Its therapeutic value is evident from a single verse taken from Hebrew history:

"And it came to pass, when the evil spirit from God was upon Saul, that David took an harp, and played with his hand: so Saul was refreshed, and was well, and the evil spirit departed from him."

Today many of our mental hospitals are experimenting with recorded music (passively heard) or vocal and instrumental music actively performed by patients. Some years ago a talented harpist told me how a simple folk tune broke the barrier of stolid indifference set up by a soldier at Lyons Veterans Hospital in New Jersey, and the associations aroused by the music brought him into relationship with the world around him so that doctors could continue to help him, now aided by his cooperation.[61]

His closing words clearly illustrate his meaning and ours:

The doctor was only partly correct in answering Macbeth's query about his wife, a rather desperate query, under the circumstances:

Canst thou not minister to a mind diseased,
Pluck from the memory a rooted sorrow,
Raze out the written troubles of the brain,
And with some sweet oblivious antidote
Cleanse the stuff'd bosom of that perilous stuff
Which weighs upon the heart?

(Doctor) Therein the patient
Must minister to himself.

And so he must. But there is given for help man's most creative art. Music *can* minister, pluck out a rooted sorrow, cleanse the heart. When it is allied with the poetry of Christian devotion, we call the result a hymn. Blessed is the pastor who knows how to use hymn tunes with understanding, for he shall let music help him minister to minds diseased, and bring its curative power to all who sing and hear.[62]

As Dr. B. A. Norris tells us: "Therapeutic value is found in coming into an awareness of God through the active participation in the singing of hymns.[63]

Dr. Blackwood emphasizes:

In music, as in everything else, the Christian minister should be a practical idealist. So he should think of the place of worship as the sanctuary. Some day perhaps he will visit the Bird Sanctuary at the Bok Memorial Tower in Florida. There, amid the trees and the music of the birds, he will find a modest board with an inscription borrowed from John Burroughs— an inscription which shows why many a strong man or weary woman comes to church and enjoys the music.

> I come here to find myself;
> it is so easy to get lost
> in the world.[64]

Music, in addition to its value as music, offers opportunities for artistic release and creative effort, and when it is produced by the joint work of groups, as in orchestras and choruses, it is the occasion for developing the co-operative attitudes and skills which are essential to the success of this type of common action throughout life. Furthermore, by their singing and playing, children and young people can provide a unique service to folk who are crippled or aged or sick which may be of great significance in promoting happy and fruitful interrelations.[65]

In closing we quote John Armstrong regarding the therapy of music:

> Sweet music
> Music exalts each joy, allays each grief,
> Expels diseases, softens every pain,
> Subdues the rage of poison, and the plague.[66]

119

1. Brooks Atkinson (ed.), *The Complete Essays and Other Writings of Ralph Waldo Emerson*, (New York: Random House, Inc., 1940), p. 5.

2. Caroline Miles Hill (ed.), *The World's Great Religious Poetry*, (New York: The Macmillan Co., 1942), p. 699, Lines 1-2.

3. *Ibid.*

4. *Ibid.*

5. Holy Bible, K.J.V., Isaiah 54:2.

6. Geo. Lyman Kittredge (ed.) *The Complete Works of Shakespeare*, (Boston: Ginn & Co., 1936), *Hamlet*, Act III, Scene ii, Line 12.

7. Washington Gladden, *The Christian Pastor and the Working Church*, (New York: Charles Scribner's Sons, 1909), p. 151.

8. William Robinson, *The Biblical Doctrine of the Church*, (St. Louis: The Bethany Press, 1948), p. 135.

9. *Ibid.*

10. Everett C. Parker, Elinor Inman, and Ross Snyder, *Religious Radio: What to Do and How*, (New York: Harper & Bros. Pub., 1948), p. 58.

11. *Ibid.*, p. 172.

12. *Ibid.*

13. J. S. Whale, *Christian Doctrine*, (Cambridge at the University Press: The Syndics of the Cambridge University Press, 1950), p. 153. Copyright: Cambridge University Press, New York.

14. *Ibid.*

15. Edgar N. Jackson, "The Therapeutic Function in Preaching," *Pastoral Psychology*, June, 1950, p. 36.

16. *Ibid.*

* With the exception of quotations reprinted from works in the public domain all excerpts are used by special permission of the present copyright holders.

17. Charles Reynolds Brown, *The Art Of Preaching*, (New York: The Macmillan Co., 1948), p. 2.

18. *Holy Bible*, K.J.V., John 14:12.

19. *Ibid*.

20. *Ibid.*, John 10:30.

21. *Ibid.*, Mark 10:18.

22. *Ibid.*, Matthew 26:53.

23. Karl A. Menninger, "Religious Applications of Psychiatry," *Pastoral Psychology*, April, 1950, p. 15.

24. Wayne E. Oates, "The Diagnostic Use of the Bible," *Pastoral Psychology*, December, 1950, p. 46.

25. Luther Allan Weigle, *Jesus and The Educational Method* (New York: The Abingdon Press, 1939), p. 18.

26. *Ibid.*, p. 32.

27. George A. Coe, *What Is Christian Education?* (New York: Charles Scribner's Sons, 1929), p. 218.

28. *Holy Bible*, K.J.V., Matthew 18:3.

29. Edward Scribner Ames, *The Psychology of Religious Experience*, (Boston: Houghton Mifflin Co., 1910), p. 258. Copyright: Harker and Brothers, New York.

30. *Ibid.*, p. 273.

31. *WTCD*, Webster's Twentieth Century Dictionary, published by the World Publishing Company, Cleveland Ohio.

32. Seward Hiltner, *Pastoral Counseling*, (New York: Abingdon Cokesbury Press, 1949), pp. 223-224. Copyright: The Abingdon Press, Nashville, Tenn.

33. Gladden, *op. cit.*, p. 157.

34. *Ibid.*, p. 158.

35. Coe, *op. cit.*, p. 41.

36. Gladden, *op. cit.*, p. 167.

37. Robinson, *op. cit.*, pp. 58-59.

38. *Ibid.*, pp. 70-71.

39. Louis Duane Hatfield, "Significance of Baptism," *The Christian Evangelist*, (now, *The Christian*), October 17, 1945, pp. 1006-1007. Published by the Christian Board of Publication, St. Louis, Mo.)

40. Whale, *op. cit.*, p. 153.

41. *Ibid.*

42. *Ibid.*, p. 91.

43. James Black, *The Mystery of Preaching*, (New York: Fleming H. Revell Co., 1924), p. 200.

44. *Ibid.*

45. Kirby Page, *Living Prayerfully*, (New York: Farrar & Rinehart, Inc., 1941), p. 1.

46. George A. Buttrick, *Prayer*, (New York: Abingdon Cokesbury Press, 1942), p. 51.

47. Horace Bushnell, *Christian Nurture*, (New Haven: Yale University Press, 1947), pp. 335-336. Copyright: The Abingdon Press, Nashville.

48. George A. Buttrick, *Jesus Came Preaching*, (New York: Charles Scribner's Sons) p. 78. Copyright 1931 Charles Scribner's Sons; renewal copyright 1959 George A. Buttrick.

49. *Ibid.*, p. 109-110.

50. *Ibid.*, p. 188-189.

51. Buttrick, *Prayer, op. cit.*, p. 53.

52. *Ibid.*, p. 303.

53. Eugene L. Smith, "The Lord's Prayer in Pre-Marital Counseling," *Pastoral Psychology*, October, 1950, p. 34.

54. Luther E. Woodward, "Contributions of the Minister to Mental Hygiene," *Pastoral Psychology*, May, 1950, p. 45.

55. Clifton E. Kew and Clinton J. Kew, "Group Psychotherapy In a Church Setting," *Pastoral Psychology*, January, 1951, p. 31.

56. Charles Dreisoerner, *The Psychology of Liturgical Music*, (Kirkwood, Mo.: Maryhurst Press, 1945), p. 155.

57. Ira M. Altshuler, "Four Years' Experience With Music as a Therapeutic Agent at Eloise Hospital," *American Journal of Psychiatry*, Volume 100, No. 7, May, 1944, pp. 792-793-794.

58. Joseph N. Ashton, *Music in Worship*, (Boston: The Pilgrim Press, 1943), p. 8.

59. Alfred B. Haas, "The Therapeutic Value of Hymns," *Pastoral Psychology*, December, 1950, p. 39.

60. *Ibid.*, p. 42.

61. Alfred B. Haas, "Hymn Tunes and Emotions," *Pastoral Psychology*, December, 1951, p. 27-28.

62. *Ibid.*, p. 30.

63. Statement by Dr. B. A. Norris, personal interview.

64. Andrew W. Blackwood, *The Fine Art of Public Worship*, (Nashville: Cokesbury Press, 1939), p. 108.

65. Hugh Hartshorne, *Character in Human Relations*, (New York: Charles Scribner's Sons, 1932), pp. 344-345.

66. H. L. Mencken (ed.), *A New Dictionary of Quotations*, (New York: Alfred A. Knopf, 1942), p. 825—Quoting John Armstrong: *The Art of Preserving Health*, IV, 1744.

Chapter 2

THE THERAPEUTICS OF COUNSELING

Introduction

If there is to be a therapy in counseling there must be some basic understanding brought to bear upon the thinking of both the counselor and the counselee. The counseling pastor is in a sense a practicing psychologist. Paul E. Johnson explains his thought that, as a practicing psychologist, Jesus was a physician of souls:

> Jesus, from our point of view was a practicing psychologist who employed psychology for practical ends in understanding persons and working with them in creative relationships. The practicing psychologist today approaches persons in three ways: (1) psychodiagnosis to discover the condition of the psyche or soul; (2) psychodynamics to understand the deep inner causes or motives of the person, and (3) psychotherapy to heal psychic conflicts and distresses in larger wholeness.[1]

Now if there is to be a psychotherapy, which we understand to be in essence a process of helping a person mature, some understanding of self and ideals is valuable, not alone to the counselor but to the counselee as well. Therefore, we will be discussing in this chapter these basic understandings of self and ideals in order to afford both the counselor and the counselee a sense of rapport in their relationships of therapy. We are not attempting here to be psychologists at all. We only seek to know some simple basic premises to help fulfill the task of counseling people. The first discussion will be, "The Way Social and Biological Factors Interact to Produce and Give Form to the Self." The second will be, "The Place of Ideals in Relation to the Process of Social-Self-Integration; Having in Mind the Nature of Ideals, How They Are Developed; and How They Operate."

Kierkegaard's definition of dread gives us the keynote reason for the felt need of counseling and the importance therefore of an understanding of self and ideals in order to mature successfully. We quote:

> Dread is the possibility of freedom. Only this dread is by the aid of faith absolutely educative, laying bare as it does all finite aims and discovering all their deceptions. And no Grand Inquisitor has in readiness such terrible tortures as has dread, and no spy knows how to attack more artfully the man he suspects, choosing the instant when he is weakest, nor knows how to lay traps where he will be caught and ensnared, as dread knows how, and no sharp-witted judge knows how to interrogate, to examine the accused, as dread does, which never lets him escape, neither by diversion nor by noise, neither at work nor at play, neither by day nor by night.
> He who is educated by dread is educated by possibility, and only the man who is educated by possibility is educated in accordance with his infinity. Possibility is therefore the heaviest of all categories.[2]

Hence we would say the possibility of being mature, or coming to be mature, is a weight upon both the counselor and the counselee and necessitates the basic understandings of self and ideals in their most dramatic sense and form.

The Way Social and Biological Factors Interact to Produce and Give Form to the Self

Definitions

Our definition of social factors is one taken from Webster which defines "social" as "pertaining to society; relating to men living in society; or to the public as an aggregate body; as, social interests are concerned; social pleasures." [3] The definition of biology as given in Webster is "the science of life; the branch of science which treats of the phenomena of animals and plants with regard to their morphology, physiology, origin or development, and distribution." [4] A definition of self as found in the same source is "the individual as an object to his own reflective consciousness; a person as a distinct individual; one's individual person; the ego of metaphysicians; the man viewed by his own cognition as the subject of all his mental phenomena, the agent in his own activities, the subject of his own feelings, and the possessor of faculties and character." [5]

The definition of social factors given above is more concerned with the purely social than it is with the combination of social factors; therefore, we will look at it as those relations or factors which arise out of man living in society and the interest developed therefrom.

Biological Factors

The statement has been made that what we are is decided or determined a hundred years before we are born. If this be true, and we have sufficient reason to believe it is, then biological factors such as heredity play an important part in the production and form of our selves. This gives substance to the statement found in the *Bible* regarding "visiting the iniquity of the fathers upon the children, and upon the children's children, unto the third, and the fourth generation." [6] If the iniquities are visited upon the children unto the fourth generation so can the better things, the goods, also be visited. There is evidence too that, regardless of the strong or weak physical nature of human beings, this strength or weakness does not necessarily determine all the activities of the self. Physical strength may serve to direct some of the efforts of the self for expression, but we all know those cases of individuals who have been weak physically and strong spiritually and mentally. Summing this up, we should remember that good health and strong bodies make for a feeling of well-being on the part of the individual. Our appetites, the things we eat, decide in a great sense what we are, because the proper diet makes the proper individual.

Another factor in this matter of biology is the one of geography. If we live in the south our feelings of push and aggressiveness are not pronounced. If we live in the temperate or more northern climates we do become and are more aggressive and active in our society. Therefore, not only do heredity and its related units affect the self, but also geography, the very place where one lives, helps direct the biological factors in the giving of form to the self.

Social Factors

Let us turn to the social aspect. The social factors are determined in a large part by whether we live in an open or closed culture. If we live in a closed culture we are victims rather than masters of ourselves, because most of our course is prescribed by the society or culture in which we live. If our habitat is an open culture we are masters of ourselves rather than victims, but in so being we assume the great responsibilities that go with the privilege.

The next step is that of environment. We must have environment in order to produce and give form to the self. For instance, we have a well, healthy, happy individual who lives in an open culture which permits him to act as a master of himself. Living in the environment we have just mentioned, he will normally respond to certain stimuli and action.

127

If that environment is controlled, and this is extremely difficult except in rural sections, his response can, in a certain sense, be determined. This is most difficult to predict if one lives in an urban environment, for within the city the stresses and strains are much more pronounced. In this issue of environment we can easily see the problems most children experience in the simple matter of growing up.

Our Responses

We now see an individual in an environment and responding to certain stimuli. These responses are positive and negative, as an electric current, in relation to his heritage, to his geography, to the culture, open or closed, within which he lives. From this response we get on the side of the biological factors certain adaptations, because of adjustments, resulting in an integration of the person or self into an individual. Now in this adaptation and adjustment social factors enter the limelight, and certain habits, ideas, motives, drives, ideals, and emotions show forth. It is through the activation of these that the self comes into being—a conscious self, if you will.

The Self

The self is the part of the individual that we come to know as it experiences relationships to social and biological factors. But the self is not just one thing. There is a self which judges itself, there is a self which is being judged, and there is a self in terms of which the judgment is being made. This consciousness of self or mind is an active potential. A person has a memory, a person has a purpose, a person has the ability to adopt a means to an end, a person has a consciousness of continuity and worth. This action of the self, or potential, which we call the mind, can rearrange and select memories. However, these memories can live only in the imagination. Hence we come to the conclusion that man knows only what he knows in his imagination. His senses perceive the outer world and conduct stimuli to his mind, the potential, where the sifting and sorting and arranging are done, resulting in a response to these stimuli. This action of the mind and this response result in what we choose to call the self or the personality.

This response to what is sent in the form of stimuli may result in inhibitions or exhibitions. The experience of the self is the determining factor here. One is either an extrovert or an introvert according to what one wills or lacks to will, resulting from past experiences of stimuli and responses. But there is a factor here which has been overlooked, and that is the spirit of this individual. This spirit is an even more finely defined thing—whatever you may call it—than the self. We can call it the unconscious or subconscious mind if we will, but it still remains as the connection between what we call God and man. The interlocking relationship between the will, the self and the spirit is often not too clearly defined. A man may will something but not have the personality, or self, to fulfill or complete it. He may have the will to do something and have the self and personality to perform it, but the spirit doesn't permit such action. Therefore it is, we believe, correct to feel, and to state, that the self is an acquirement of experience, the reaction of that self being the will. The spirit, or the mental good-feeling, is a part of that will, and the sum total of all this results in the character of an individual. These actions, and these interactions, and these reactions temper the self and the will and the spirit making an individual's character.

The Place of Ideals in Relation to the Process of Social-Self-Integration; Having in Mind the Nature of Ideals, How They Are Developed, and How They Operate

Definitions

All values are arranged in some hierarchy. For example, habits, ideas, motives, drives, ideals, and emotions are all related and are set up in some type of hierarchy. We are concerned here with ideals; this is only one of the values in the development of personality which we will discuss. Our concern is what gives direction to ideals. First let us define an ideal. We are told: "it is a statement, conception, of desired and approved possibilities, of either ends or processes, relating either to one's self or to a situation." [7] For instance, in every situation one encounters there is a response and that response is governed or controlled by what one considers the ideal. This ideal is either high or low depending on the development of the individual's ability to appreciate ideals. We have many responses to situations to which we connect no ideals at all, because we have never found it necessary, or perhaps have never taken the time, or it has never been brought to our attention by our culture, our society, our nation, our community, our church, our schools, or even our family that there must be an ideal approach to every situation and that ideal should govern our response to it. An ideal is the power of individuals to decide for themselves what is best for them. If they have never had any experience with ideals how can they know what is the ideal for a particular situation? Further, it is a cosmic warrant, a faith that such and so will happen. It is something like the farmer who sows seed and has faith that it will grow. Types of self, ideal, are pictures one has of oneself as such and so, for instance, as a hero.

Motivation

Let us consider some types of motivation which will give us the background for the nature of ideals, how they are developed, and how they operate. There are four types of motivation in regard to the response of self to a situation: first, what is the self going to get out of it? This is the egocentric type of thinking; second, the concern for others as well as self; third, complete self-abnegation or self-denial—

self gives all to the situation; fourth, the interrelationship or democratic type of response which is a mutuality, a place in the group. This last one seems to be the only effective means or motivation for the purpose of the development of ideals, that is, proper ideals. Ideals are very important in regard to personality. Ideals can be the cause of living. Is the kingdom of God an ideal? But the kingdom of God is within us. Or is the term love better? Isn't love what the New Testament is seeking?

Virtues

Personality consists of specific virtues which are achieved one by one, and the total composes the total person. The problem here is the ambiguity of terms which makes it difficult. For example, neatness and courtesy, what are these? What happens when you add all of the virtues together? What is the result? Is it a matter of kindness versus honesty? If you make a choice you are using an outside control to dictate to these specifics. Love is not an absolute. Love is not a virtue. Another difficulty is in the grading of these virtues. Sometimes adding more of a virtue to itself makes it a vice. Persistence can thus become obstinacy. Determining the ethical value of these virtuous qualities involves difficulty, for a thief must have many of the virtues of an honest citizen in order to be a successful thief. Virtues are tools then rather than ends. Besides, objectives are what really matter. Another difficulty with virtues is that instead of being concrete they are abstract. From actual behavior observed and recorded it has been found there is no correlation between these behavior patterns. Knowing what is good does not determine whether the behavior pattern would be good. To deal with a virtue by teaching it through words does not improve its value to individuals. Behavior is a function of the situation rather than the thinking of the individual in the light of his ideals.

Ideals

Ideals are transmitted by words, although this practice is discouraged—the difficulty here being, of course, that the cultivation of virtues encourages introversion. If there were no poor, what about charity? Hence objective thinking is important. Paul Vieth explains five steps in the education for ideals: "First, exposure, listening to what is to be achieved. Second, repetition, through advanced forms. Third, understanding, very important. Fourth, conviction, child thoroughly convinced to use this behavior. Fifth, application, how many different places can or has the child used this teaching?" [8] We can see that the keynote here is that desirability is talked up and it is encouraged.

Authority

Every child is in tension or conflict merely by virtue of being alive. The character of a culture is vividly displayed in its educational approach. An authority definition is one approach. The child is taken care of by the parents, the authority of expediency. If a child is dependent completely upon his parents, this is again the authority of expediency. Through obedience to natural law one can avoid difficulties. Who is or what is the authority? The authority of God? Of the church? Of education? Of experience? Is authority purely arbitrary? What authority are you going to accept? Authority of individual conscience is Protestantism. An identification of authority with power is, however, a different matter.

Integration of Ideals

How does culture transmit its values—ideals, virtues, behavior, etc.? Primarily human beings do not always respond in specific ways. Integration—what is it? Drives and urges in relation to one another are integrated. Drives and urges are integrated in regard to ideals. What is integration for? It is what maintains the survival of the individual, the balance of life. The behavior of individuals must be considered in the light of the responses found. The integration of humans, adults, is of the highest nature. An action usually follows the demand of the situation. Is integrated action the result of integrated thinking? It should be. Consistent behavior should bear study. Consistency in particular integration is true in the great majority. One half of the children are honest one half of the time. If a child will cheat in only one way it will be the easy one. The more honest are more consistent. The less honest are less consistent. Some integration seems to be the teacher of personality. A systematic performance of activities results in the theory of the hierarchy of habits. One must recognize that the nervous system is adaptable.

Character is the machine as a whole, the integrated parts. Energy must motivate this integration. There are as many different makes of persons as different makes of cars. We have brakes to stop the process of any action. We have a steering wheel to redirect action. Man is at the steering wheel and should answer where he is going! Personality is all these things. Relational action, the personality, is the relation of self to all reality. More knowledge of reality results in a more sensitive personality. No two individuals have the same world. The world is what we are able to receive. Ideals are the organizing forces of our integration. Ethical integration is what? What principle is here? Ethical integration is conscious participation with universal forces making us growing individuals. Perfect integration is only instantaneous. We are always reintegrating. Integration that is dynamic makes for a process. Not only do we adapt but we reconstruct that which caused the need for adaptation.

There is a relationship between what persons say and what they do. There is a correlation between knowledge and conduct. Is behavior a function of the group? What other people think we ought to think many times determines our thinking. Assuming that one group is ethically predominant, such as the home, church, church school, Y.M.C.A., or Boy Scouts, doesn't work out in the encouragement of ethical responsibility. How can integration be achieved in this maze of ethical jargon? One answer is a responsiveness to a general ethical concept for all groups, which is set up in the light of what they may become, not what they are. Another is social interaction which permits the growth of a person. A static or absolute approach is not effective. An integration in growth in the presence of variety is necessary. Potentiality is the determining factor in growth. The relationship of individuals and groups is what must be studied.

Function of Ideals

A concept of function is the thought here. This extension is beyond that of a biological or mechanical function: first, the machine or mechanical function; second, the biological function; third, the primitive social function; fourth, the group social function; fifth, the indeterminate function, because of environment. These systems of life have a relationship in function to each other. The penetrating wedge, ideals, through these systems of life, is governed by individual and group thought. It is in terms of what the group is doing or in terms of what the individuals are doing in relation to each other and the group.

These functions may be, first, purposefully, a social purpose, an important purpose; second, skill, an increasing skill, social skills, what people do in order to fit together, for trouble is most generally caused by a lack of adjustment to social skills; third, a sense of belonging, a social function, belonging to the group, a deliberate sense of belonging; fourth, a spirit of co-operation, an attitude of co-operation—joy is, but gloom is not, a characteristic of functioning together (an example is singing while working); fifth, meaningfulness, the setting in a larger unit. Culture is an adjustment to physical environment, cosmic and climate relationships. Should one question the drive or impulse? True social

134

function is not a veneer. A religious act is this highest concept of function in its definable and understandable form. This wedge, ideals, is the correlation or relationship of these functions, all the way from mechanical environment and function to indeterminate environment and its function.

Relation of Values

An integration of the realities of the external world with the hierarchy of values is inherent in the individual. What is our relation to these values? Religion is the wedge that penetrates these spheres of realities. Religious concern is the concern of the personality. The character of the whole reality is religion, that is the activity of religion. The washing of dishes and the shelling of peas are illustrations of a phase of reality. It is important to carry back to the beginning and end of experiences of this type to appreciate this. We must give meaning to routine tasks of daily activities or we shall suffer a great fatigue. The enjoyment of our daily lives is vital. Take a dishrag and discuss it. Surround it with an adequate understanding. Successful adjustment comes with an understanding of routine. Out of this evolves the new. The continuity of thinking is important to insure union between the past and future, resulting in the present. Values arise out of these experiences. Emergent evolution is the result of our daily living.

Potentialities

The concept of potentiality. We don't want to know what is going to happen. Predetermination by God is rather boring to him. Maintenance, reproduction, government, and education, why do we do these things? They make the usual behavior of persons who follow these patterns only into dull routine. A compensation for this machine routine is necessary. Play is the compensation for this. Most of us do not know how to play. It must be learned. These routines must be lifted to the level of religious functions. Concerns of religion are the concerns of life. Institutionalizing makes for stereotyping. Religion, when it becomes an institution, becomes a stereotype. If we were to make a chart showing the functions of maintenance, reproduction, government, and education as the blades of a propeller, adding to these blades the one of play, we would find ourselves with many short stubby blades, for our interest in some is not appreciable. If such a propeller were hooked to an airplane or used for a windmill the power developed would be quite inadequate. In like manner our lives don't develop much power. Churches instead of emancipating their people subject them to this same stereotyping of experience and thus limit their character. Devotion, concern, and love are free, while you are still a slave. You do the right thing because you wish to. Remember Paul's statement about being free while still a slave. Religion is the demand for the release of personality. It is an escape into the world of human realities. Religious concern is with social order. The common affairs of life cannot be separated from religion. Human advance is being worked out through experimentation rather than accepted as predestined. Should we stereotype the criteria? No! Let us develop the criteria. Are the Ten Commandments stereotyped? Are the Laws of Hammurabi stereotyped? We should be creators as well as creatures. Man is this.

Creative Processes

What makes people tick? The pressure of cultures is tremendous. Hence metaphysics has something to say to us. Religion is concerned with the achievement, organization, and conservation of value in connection with certain cosmic relations. In creative processes man does this. Religion is not added, but is a reality without and within. We are actually wholes—not mechanical entireties, but creative personalities,

136

resulting in individuals with character. We must have a functional relationship with this totality called God. Our entireties must be related to this totality called God. This is the religious quality or character of life. Religion is not a generic force in human life. It is a development rather than a manifestation. The universe has an attitude toward us. We have an attitude toward the universe. Psychology is concerned with the latter. In the realm of the metaphysical we have three positions: first, any attitude toward the supernatural; second, any special attitude towards the supernatural; third, any special attitudes towards any special kind of supernatural. In the realm of the psychological we have two positions: one, any attitude towards life; two, any attitude toward a special attitude. Reverence towards God is reverence; but it is not when directed toward anything else.

Objectives Acquired Through Experience

The object is what makes anything religious. An uneasiness, then a solution—that is religion. Religion is the whole process of going from one phase to another. "The consciousness of the highest social values" [9] is Ames' definition of religion. The principle of policy we give ourselves to, love of love, is the Johannean position. Dr. Luther Weigle holds four variances of religious experience: first, human wants, desires, drives, etc., what we want; second, powers beyond our control, the attitude of the universe towards us; third, working programs between the above two; fourth, an emergent revaluation of the whole above experience. [10]

Religion demands not an object, but an arena with the capacity for action, the action of values. The relationship between the ideal and the actual is religion. Religion demands a potentiality, action therefrom results in character. Hence we say there is a therapy in counseling, both for the counselor and the counselee, particularly when it is based upon such basic understandings of self and ideals.

137

Notes *

1. Paul E. Johnson, "Jesus As Psychologist," *Pastoral Psychology*, December, 1951, p. 18.
2. Søren Aabye Kierkegaard, *The Concept of Dread*, Translated by Walter Lowrie (Princeton University Press, 1946), pp. 139-140.
3. *WTCD*, Webster's Twentieth Century Dictionary.
4. *Ibid.*
5. *Ibid.*
6. *Holy Bible*, K.J.V., Exodus 34:7.
7. Statement by Dr. Hugh Hartshorne, in class lecture at Yale.
8. Statement by Dr. Paul H. Vieth, in class lecture at Yale.
9. Edward Scribner Ames, *The Psychology of Religious Experience*, (Boston: Houghton Mifflin Co., 1910), p. viii.
10. Statement by Dr. Luther Weigle, in class lecture at Yale.

* With the exception of quotations reprinted from works in the public domain all excerpts are used by special permission of the present copyright holders.

Chapter 3

THE THERAPEUTICS OF RELIGIOUS DRAMA

Introduction

It is far more satisfying to me to recognize that human beings are born into a personal relationship; that they attain the essentially human traits through interaction with groups of persons; that their minds are so shaped and fashioned in conversation that it is with difficulty and the most arduous training that they ever approximate genuinely "abstract" thinking, and then only in a very limited field of reflection, and only for short periods of the day; that in their families and among their friends and as members of social organizations they are living in vivid personal ways and thinking in the imagery of persons; and that in religion they tend to dramatize their relation to Life itself, and to regard themselves as in communion with the great heart of the world, humanized and personified in the character of God.[1]

With this quotation from Dr. Ames' "My Conception of God" we introduce this chapter on religious drama and its therapeutic values. In this paragraph quotation we note he states, "in religion they tend to dramatize their relation to Life itself,"[2] as he goes about explaining how man conducts himself and does his thinking. Apparently Dr. Ames is seeking to tell us that man at the very heart of his thinking, particularly his religious thinking, does it in a dramatic way and in a dramatic pattern. This would, or should, lead us to appreciate there must be a therapy in drama, religious or otherwise.

What Therapy Is Found in Religious Drama?

Dr. Eastman, in his book, *Drama in the Church*, has this to say under the subject, "What Drama Can Contribute":

Two examples will illustrate what drama can contribute to the culture of the human spirit. The first is from ancient Greece. For nearly five hundred years the Athenians made drama their chief means of adult religious education. They housed it in their most sacred temple. They presented their greatest dramas there at the sacred season of the year. They closed their places of business, adjourned their courts, and even opened their jails so that everyone might come and receive the intellectual and spiritual stimulus of the plays. So powerful was the effect of those religious dramas that Athenians developed an understanding and an insight which made their names a symbol of culture from that day to this. Read those plays today— the dramas of Aeschylus, Sophocles, and Euripides especially—and you will see why they have lived for twenty-four hundred years. There is life in them, and a striving after truth, and there is supreme beauty.

Another example is that of the Canterbury cathedral. Several years ago it decided to produce a religious drama at Christmas time. It considered the possible playwrights, selected England's leading poet, John Masefield, and asked him to write a poetic drama, "The Coming of Christ." Next it asked Gustav Holst, a foremost composer, to create the music. Then it secured the best available players, singers, and director. The result was a play of power and beauty that will

140

probably live as long as the English language lives. That is taking drama seriously.

How can modern American churches achieve through religious drama results comparable to those of the Greeks or of the Canterbury cathedral? By treating it with the same respect. By cultivating it in our temples. By giving it the best equipment, not the worst. By encouraging our best dramatists and players to consecrate at least a part of their talents to Christian service. By putting our younger players and playwrights through a rigorous discipline. By choosing the best plays, not the cheapest. By entrusting drama, not to the immature, but to those whose own struggles have brought to them that refinement of spirit essential to a sympathetic portrayal of human character in action.[3]

The challenge above, hurled at the churches by Dr. Eastman, is certainly worthy of consideration. It should lift our sights above what they are and have been. In speaking of the process of growth in the use of drama within the churches under the topic, "A New Definition of Religious Drama," he says:

In this evolution the experiences of the churches gradually gave a new definition to religious drama. In the beginning it was somehow felt that a religious drama must talk much about religion, and about Christ and the church; it must use biblical characters and to a large extent biblical stories. But in the course of the years we have come to see that what makes a play religious is not the material it deals with but *the total effect of the play upon the audience.* If a play sends an audience away exalted in spirit, with a deeper sense of fellowship with God and man, it has been religious. But if it does not have that effect it is not religious

141

although all its characters are biblical and its story taken from the Bible itself. The churches have presented many an irreligious Bible play, and the theatres many a religious modern one. *Jephthah's Daughter* is a fair example of an irreligious biblical play, while Shaw's *St. Joan, Outward Bound* by Vane, *R.U.R.* by Capek, *Our Town*, by Thornton Wilder, *The Corn is Green*, by Emlyn Williams, and *The Family Portrait*, by Coffee and Cowen are examples of modern plays that have a religious effect.[4]

Further, he states the real and basic reason for drama in the church:

They are using it in a deliberate attempt to develop strength, beauty, and power in the imaginative and creative life of the players and the audiences.[5]

Later he again emphasizes his point when he speaks of "The Decisive Religious Test" in determining the religious value of any good play:

The religious value of any good play is determined solely by the total effect which it has upon the audience which sees it and the actors who produce it. The mere fact that a play happens to be biblical or that its characters chance to live in Palestine does not guarantee its religious nature. Nor does the fact that its locale is a mission field or a modern church.

But if, as a result of seeing the play, the men and women in the audience are lifted closer to God and inspired to go out and live more Christ-like lives, then the play is a religious play. So, too, with the actors. If the interpretation of their roles broadens their sympathies and purifies their hearts by a sense of the sacredness of life, then the play is a religious play. Religious drama must meet this pragmatic test of the effect it has upon both audience and players before it is entitled to the name.[6]

He, Dr. Eastman, is not alone in this thinking. In the March, 1952 issue of *Theatre Arts*, Helen Hayes writes:

A great play will always have two things—a certain quality which reflects its country and period of origin, and a certain usefulness to a great many people that we might call universality. For this reason the theatre is an important medium for promoting understanding between men of different nations, for audiences are led to appreciate through the drama both the life and culture of a country other than their own, and they also learn that human nature itself is pretty much the same the world over. It is revealing and uplifting for an audience to discover its own problems, passions, and aspirations mirrored in the plays of Shakespeare, Moliere and Ibsen.[7]

The key to all this is put forward by Michael Chekhov when he discusses what an actor must have and delineates the feeling of compassion as being of vital importance to the actor in an article in the *Theatre Arts* for December, 1952:

The other attribute of creative feelings is that they are compassionate. Your higher self endows the character with creative feelings; and because it is able at the same time to observe its creation, it has compassion for its characters and their destinies. Thus the true artist in you is able to suffer for Hamlet, cry with Juliet, laugh about the mischief-making of Falstaff.

Compassion may be called the fundamental of all good art because it alone can tell you what other beings feel and experience. Only compassion severs the bonds of your personal limitations and gives you deep access into the inner life of the character you study, without which you cannot properly prepare it for the stage.[8]

Where and When Is There a Therapy of Religious Drama?

In keeping with the acceptance of Dr. Eastman's challenge regarding the value of drama for the development of the culture of the human spirit, we turn now to some examples of the realization of such an effort. Henry Hewes, in an article, "The Drama Prospers in Pittsburgh," reports:

> To most theatregoers Pittsburgh is merely the place where Eleonora Duse died. Actually, however, the city has outgrown such transient importance, not so much because of the many successful actors who have emerged from its environs, nor from the old Nixon theatre which was a road-show stronghold for half a century, but from what best can be described as a unique and healthy working situation that has flourished between the Carnegie Tech drama department, the first college to give a bachelor's degree in the drama, and the Pittsburgh Playhouse, as prosperous a community theatre as can be found in the United States.
>
> Carnegie Tech, which inaugurated its drama department in 1914 with a class of eighteen students, now has an enrollment of 165 and presents six major productions a year, each performed ten times in its 400-seat theatre. Its audience is limited to students and faculty, 600 patrons (there is a long waiting list of people wishing to become patrons) and outsiders who come and queue up on the chance that there may be some vacant seats.[9]

Under its department, "Theatre Off-Broadway," the April issue for 1952 of the *Theatre Arts* explains "What *Murder in the Cathedral* Did to Garden City":

144

An inspired theatre with four performances of *Murder in the Cathedral* has succeeded in transforming the social atmosphere of Garden City, New York. Adelphi College's production in the Episcopalian Cathedral of Incarnation, brought together various denominations and social groups, and cemented relations between the college and the community, a feat which no other cultural activity had previously accomplished.

From the success of this production, Adelphi officials conclude that cooperative theatrical projects are an invaluable means of achieving mutual understanding and interest between colleges and their surrounding communities.[10]

In *Theatre Arts* under the department, "Theatre Off-Broadway," is this report:

Pastor Leads Footlighters

Between sermons, the Rev. Frank Butterworth, pastor of the White Temple Church of Anaheim, California, directs a traveling drama troupe which he organized several years ago. The group, called Footlighters of the White Temple Church, is a definite part of the church's year-round program of Christian education for youth.

According to Mr. Butterworth, "Some men like to play golf, some like to paint or work in the garden. For ten years the production of religious plays has been a hobby with me. I'd rather do my playing with growing youngsters because I am convinced that this is a good way of educating youth in biblical events and leading our players on to successful leadership in colleges and universities."

The White Temple Church sends out a road show each year, made up of capable young players. The best roles are alternated so that no star complex is formed by any of the group.

The troupe makes trips at vacation times—Christmas, Easter and in the summer. Victoria, B. C., saw them two years ago; last year they played on a number of northern California stages; and this year they went to Arizona.

Collections are taken at the performances, and these usually cover the cost of a week's tour. Whenever a profit is made, it is donated to a youth cause. This year the extra amount was sent to Camp Kailani in Hawaii.

A play that has proved popular is Vivian Johannes' study of Pontius Pilate called *The Cup of Trembling*.[11]

In the realm of Passion Plays some of the outstanding in the United States are: *The Black Hills Passion Play*, the *Pageant* presented each Easter at Lawton, Oklahoma, of the *Life of Christ*, *The Original American Passion Play* at Bloomington, Illinois, and *From Manger to Throne* at East Haven, Connecticut. All of these of course stem from the Oberammergau production in Germany. The Bloomington, Illinois, and the East Haven, Connecticut ones will be dealt with under our next topic. Suffice it to say in closing that the therapy of religious drama is no respecter of where and when, but only of the fact of religious drama itself being performed.

How Is There a Therapy in Religious Drama and Who is Involved?

The Original American Passion Play, Bloomington, Illinois

In a letter to Dr. P. C. Somerville, Secretary of this production group, dated November 5, 1952, certain questions were asked him regarding the conduct of this play. Following are listed the questions. After each question is the answer received from him. These replies were made in his letter dated November 13, 1952, addressed to the writer:

Question 1. What use is made of the funds taken in at the box-office?

Answer: Funds are used to pay necessary expenses.

Question 2. Are any of the actors or actresses paid?

Answer: No.

Question 3. What relationship exists between the production of the play and the Masonic Temple in which it is produced?

Answer: The Passion Play is produced and presented under the auspices of the Scottish Rite Bodies of Bloomington, Illinois, and is presented on the stage in the Temple's auditorium.

Question 4. Is the play produced for the spiritual uplift of the audience or the cast?

Answer: Produced only for the spiritual up-lift for the people who witness it and naturally those who participate in it can be spiritually aided.

Question 5. Are the actors or actresses required to be members of the Masonic Order or the Eastern Star in order to participate?

Answer: No, and I may add that Protestants, Jews, and Catholics participate in the presentation of the American Passion Play.

Question 6. Is anyone in the community, who is qualified histrionically, permitted to take part?

Answer: Yes.

Question 7. What relationships exist between the churches of the community and the Passion Play? [12]

Answer: None, definitely, but I have never heard of a Protestant, Jewish, or Catholic Church of the Community, this State or adjoining states, which does not look on the American Passion Play with great acceptance.[13]

147

"From Manger to Throne," A Pageant of the Life of Jesus Christ As Presented in East Haven, Connecticut

We have been trying to show, under this topic, the bearing creative group experience has on religious growth. In dealing with the Original American Passion Play, Bloomington, Illinois, we used the question and answer approach. In regard to "From Manger to Throne" we will endeavor to recount the experience.

"From Manger to Throne" in its entirety deals with the experience of more than two hundred people in the presentation of a drama of the life of Jesus Christ.

> *Ingredients:* An idea, Religious drama. The life of Jesus Christ.
> A group of consecrated people.
> Some encouragement.
> A lot of cooperation.
> *Results:* A Pageant of the Life of Jesus Christ.
> A fellowship.
> A community.
> Drama does minister to the growth of the community.

An idea. The possibility of presenting the Twentieth Year of the Pageant of the Life of Jesus Christ, "From Manger to Throne," in the writer's community was made known. Religious drama has always been utilized by the Roman Catholic Church in its ministry with emphasis upon the passion of Christ. Here was the opportunity for not only this ministry to be afforded, but for the entire life of Jesus Christ to be depicted.

A group of consecrated people. To set aside, to tap on the shoulder if you will, more than two hundred people to be willing to make the effort for such an undertaking, was necessary. One hundred and twenty people were needed in the cast alone. In addition, there was needed a wardrobe group of twenty-five, a make-up department of another twenty-five, and a stage crew of more than that number. Here was a challenge. It was met in this way.

Some encouragement. People need help; they need a friendly hand on their shoulder. These things they want. These things they will have or go elsewhere. Every new member and those old members who could see the challenge were enlisted in the work and plans for this effort. "Here, my friend, is a chance for you to give of your time and talents for the ministry of education through the medium of religious drama." "But," was the reply, "I am no actor." Still, through the gentle means of encouragement, they did become actors, actresses, carpenters, lighting experts, make-up artists, costume makers, yea, singers of better calibre than ever before. How did they do this?

A lot of cooperation. The "coo" of the dove of peace is more powerful than the mailed fist of force. This experience proved that to more than two hundred people.

A Pageant of the Life of Jesus Christ was one of the results. Here was a religious drama, a copy of the original, that did more to those two hundred people participating than any experience they ever had before. Here were men and women, boys and girls, enacting the very drama of the one we all hold dear as he moved among people just like them in that far-off day. Not only were they guided into a new experience, but all who beheld the work of their hands and minds were likewise guided to new light.

A fellowship was another result of this experience. The fellowship thus created felt the stress and strain, not only of their own human emotions, but those of the characters they portrayed. They came to know that Jesus Christ walked and talked with men and women, boys and girls just like them, and that he had answers for their problems just as he did for those in that far-off day. This feeling came to be so pronounced that on the opening night as well as during the dress rehearsal the cast found themselves stunned into silence when they faced the figure of Jesus Christ as he walked and talked

149

with them. Time and time again there were long pauses while senses were collected and the drama moved on in its simplicity and humility. This feeling was transmitted to the witnessing audience and they too were captured by the spell and followed in utter submission of thought and action the enactment of the life of the very son of God.

A community was another result of this religion drama. From this fellowship the community of the children of God was felt by all involved in the experience, both by those in the performance and by those witnessing it. For Roman Catholics, Protestants, and Jews were in attendance, both in the cast and in the audience. Here was re-created the original community. Here men, women, and children were first children of God. Here true love was made manifest in the ministry of time and talents for those in the cast and production company and the ministry of possessions for those who came and purchased seats for the occasion. All shared in a uniting experience.

Drama does minister to the growth of the community. Let it be known that creative group experience has a great bearing on religious growth. The writer can bear witness to the fact that it does. He knew these people both before and after this group experience. He cannot emphasize too much the fact that the experience must be of a group nature and that it must be a creative one. At this vantage point the writer is confident time will prove this contention. For the sake of the work of the Church and the ministry of the word of God alone we pray this will be true. Never underestimate the power of drama in the life and growth of the religious community.

In reply to an inquiry to the University Church of Disciples of Christ in Chicago, Illinois, the pastor, Irvin E. Lunger, wrote a letter telling of the many uses of drama in the heavy schedule of that great church. We quote a paragraph from his informative letter which concerns the value of drama in the church:

Drama serves a most important function in the church. It involves a cross-section of members in a creative enterprise. It stimulates the imagination and calls forth considerable study and thought. It lifts moments of celebration and observance to impressive levels. In drama religion rises above creed and formal expression and finds voice and action in a freer realm.[14]

Notes *

1. Edward Scribner Ames, "My Conception of God," *Contemporary Religious Thought, An Anthology*, Compiled by Thomas S. Kepler, (New York: Abingdon Cokesbury Press, 1941), p. 183.
2. *Ibid.*
3. Fred Eastman and Louis Wilson, *Drama in the Church*, (New York: Samuel French, Inc., 1942), pp. 6-7 pp. 17-18. Copyright, 1933, by Samuel French; Revised Edition, Copyright, 1942, by Samuel French; Copyright (In Renewal), 1960, by Fred Eastman. All rights reserved. Reprinted by permission of the authors and Samuel French.
4. *Ibid.*, pp. 17-18.
5. *Ibid.*, p. 18.
6. *Ibid.*, pp. 23-24.
7. Helen Hayes, "Theatre for the World," *Theatre Arts*, March, 1952, p. 31.
8. Michael Chekhov, "An Actor Must Have Three Selves," *Theatre Arts*, December, 1952, p. 32.
9. Henry Hewes, "The Drama Prospers in Pittsburgh," *Theatre Arts*, October, 1952, p. 53.
10. "Theatre Off-Broadway" Dept., "What *Murder in*

the Cathedral Did to Garden City," *Theatre Arts*, April, 1952, p. 94.

11. "Theatre Off-Broadway" Dept., "Pastor Leads Footlighters," *Theatre Arts*, November, 1952, p. 84.

12. Questions asked in letter to P. C. Somerville, Ph.D., Sec. American Passion Play, Bloomington, Illinois, November 5, 1952.

13. Answers received from P. C. Somerville, Ph.D., Sec. American Passion Play, Bloomington, Illinois, November 13, 1952.

14. Letter from the Reverend Irvin E. Lunger, Pastor of the University Church of Disciples of Christ, Chicago, Illinois, August 8, 1952.

Chapter 4

CONCLUSION

The Therapeutic Theatre

Dr. J. L. Moreno, the foremost authority in this field of
the therapeutic theatre, is our teacher here as he speaks to us
in this fashion:

> In our time, in the last twenty-five years, a new
> revolution took place when the first therapeutic theatre
> was started in Vienna. It was again due to a radical
> change of operation. The method has become known
> as psychodrama, sociodrama, role playing, and action
> taking. *The patient is now an actor on the stage, acting
> before a smaller or larger audience of other patients.*
> The physician-patient relation has become subsidiary.
> Again, we are in the midst of an overhauling of theory.
> With the new operation, new concepts and theories
> are emerging. It consists of two procedures: (a) treat-
> ment of the audience (group psychotherapy); (b)
> representatives of the group portray on the stage the
> problem which disturbs the audience (action ther-
> apy). The group is facing the mirror of itself (in many
> versions) on the stage. It looks into this mirror and
> sees itself. The responses coming from the shock to the
> audio ego (members of tthe audience) and to the
> auxiliary egos (actors on the stage) are systematically
> followed up.[1]

The Meaning of the Therapeutic Theatre

Here again, Dr. Moreno is our teacher as he explains his position as to the meaning of the therapeutic theatre:

> But this mad passion, this unfoldment of life in the domain of illusion does not work like a renewal of suffering, rather it confirms the rule; every *true* second time is the liberation from the first. Liberation is an exaggerated definition of what takes place because complete repetition of a process makes its subject look foolish or ridiculous. One gains towards his own life, towards all one has done and does, *the point of view of the creator*—the experience of the true freedom, the freedom from his own nature. The first time brings the second time to laughter. One speaks, eats, drinks, procreates, sleeps, is awake, writes, fights, quarrels, earns, loses, dies the second time too—in psychodramatic ways. But the same pain does not affect the player and spectator as pain, the same want does not affect him as want, the same thought does not affect him as thought. It is painless, consciousless, thoughtless, deathless. Every living figure denies and resolves itself through psychodrama. Life and psychodrama offset each other and go under in laughter. It is the final form of the theatre.[2]

Dramatics Program at VA Hospital

Patients with mental illnesses in the Veterans Administration hospital at Coatesville, Pa., are taking part in a program of dramatics which, in addition to acting, includes training in property making, costume designing, scenery designing, casting, directing, and script writing. Several one-act and three-act comedies and dramas and a musical review have been presented in the hospital auditorium; and small units within the theatre group have given a number of skits for the entertainment of fellow-patients unable to leave their wards.

The dramatic program is under the direction of Mrs. Carolin Witherspoon, a volunteer worker associated with the American Theatre Wing, who during the war organized similar programs in army hospitals.[3]

Summary

Under the topics, "The Therapeutic Theatre," "The Meaning of the Therapeutic Theatre," and "Dramatics Program at VA Hospital" we have sought to project the thought, through the minds of those qualified to speak on the subject, that regardless of the medium of expression, whether it be television, radio, films, or the stage, the utilizing of professional artists cannot exercise a complete therapeutical assistance to individuals in distress mentally and emotionally. The amateur, the one needing help, can be helped more through actual participation on his own part.

In presenting ideas and helps to those in need of them there are several methods of approach which we will present after we make the suggestion that there is much to be said for films and mental health. Every church and pastor should be familiar with the potentialities available through films. This is underscored by Cecile Starr in "Films and Mental Health" in *Pastoral Psychology*, in the opening sentence of the article: "In the past few years, mental health has almost completely dominated the documentary film world." [4]

Now we turn to several ways of dramatically presenting ideas and aids to those in need of them.

Speech or Film. This is by far the most commonly used type of presentation method. Included are the guest expert who presents some special information; the dynamic speaker who stimulates, arouses, or sets the tone for the meeting; the big name who acquaints the audience with his personality or point of view; the humorist or artist who entertains the audience. The documentary film or speech, when used primarily to supply information or express a point of view, may also be included here.

Panel, symposium, forum. This category includes methods in which several persons are brought together to give information or engage in controversy. Examples are the symposium in which several speakers are combined with a chairman; the panel in which participants interact with one another and the discussion is guided by a moderator; the forum or its variant, the Town Hall presentation, in which two or more speakers take opposing sides on an issue and a moderator summarizes points of view and leads the audience discussion.

Speaker with visual exhibit. Here we find a speaker with auxiliary visual aids. Book or easel type of charts, turnover talks or flip-flops, may illustrate processes, reinforce points, etc. Animated or silhouette charts which make use of a magnetic or flannel board allow the speaker to build the units of the visual as he speaks. A vuegraph, a machine which projects what the operator draws or writes on a transparent surface, allows the speaker to prepare visual aids on the spot in the course of his presentation. Models, displays, or movable exhibits give three-dimensional perspective. Slides, film-strips, and movies can also be used in conjunction with the speaker.

Presenting an action situation. This type of presentation shows people acting in such a way as to illuminate the situation in which the action occurs. Role playing, case-study presentations, and staged or filmed vignettes are examples. A commentator or narrator may be used with any of these methods to call the attention of the audience to specific points.

Dramatizing a conflict. Conflict presentations point up the outer or inner forces which clash with each other in a human situation. Role playing, staged skits, filmed or danced presentations which highlight conflict are examples. Vivid portrayal of inner conflict may be provided by alter-ego and ghost voice presentations. The former method employs two persons for each character. One person speaks publicly for the character. The alter-ego, who usually stands behind the public person, verbalizes inner thoughts and feelings. The ghost voice, presented through an off-stage microphone, can be used in conjunction with an on-stage character to express the conscience of the character. A recorded skit acompanied by pantomine is another way to dramatize conflict.

Demonstrating a skill or technique. This type includes presentations of an action by film or live actors. Its essential characteristic is that it focuses on the techniques or skills to be used in dealing with a situation. Skills demonstrated may be as simple as a dance step or as complex as leading a committee to a decision. Contrasting ways of meeting a situation are presented and the audience is asked to discuss the similarities and differences, the advantages and disadvantages of the two ways.

A great preacher offers this admonition, to those who would encourage the catharsis and therapy which the ministry of music affords in worship. We quote Perry E. Gresham:

> Music as we know it was born in the Church. Yet today the scourge of syncopated tunes and slushy or unworthy words has smitten the people of God. A concert psychology has infected the choirs and sentimentalism has corrupted the taste of the worshipers. The perpetuation of bad musical art can be partly charged to the clergy. The Christian world awaits some genius who can do for our day what Bach or Palestrina did for theirs. In the meantime, it behooves the minister to know the difference between worthy and unworthy hymns and anthems in order that he might better lead his flock to "worship the Lord in the beauty of holiness" and not in the ugliness of mistaken piety.

Drama is closely allied to worship. The Lord Himself chose the dramatic triumphal entry into Jerusalem as the medium by which to declare His Messiahship. The simple drama in the Upper Room is the central core of the Christian tradition. The play, like other arts, was mothered by religion. An effective drama speaks a deep and primitive religious message. The minister who understands the nature of ceremonials and can develop them so that they carry tension and surprise in high dignity has found an important clue to the most effective way to proclaim the Christian message. Seminary students might learn more from Shakespeare superbly presented than from some required reading. There is no more effective nor delightful way for a minister to gain insight into life than for him to attend a good play.[5]

In closing we look to Joseph Fort Newton, who suggests that all our questions cannot be answered here and now when he says:

> How many tangles all of us would like to unravel, but it is impossible. At times, if we are patient and lucky and get hold of the right thread, a knot that looked hopeless can be untwisted; but it is not always so.
>
> Here Shakespeare can help us. In his early plays the action is decided and completed within the play, all issues settled. In later plays it is less so, albeit the divinity appears at the end to adjust inequalities.
>
> But when we reach the great tragedies like *Hamlet*, *Othello*, and *King Lear*, the situation has become too complex and involved to be neatly closed and finished; the problem is pushed forward into "the beyond."
>
> If there were no "beyond," where errors are corrected and injustices are revised, where questions are answered and bitter sorrows are healed, how ghastly, how heavy and intolerable human life would be.
>
> What, then, are we to do when life gets tangled? Give up and let things go, like the man in the parable?

No, we must try to undo the wrong we have done and atone for unwise words and acts.

But if by so trying to make good an error we do more harm than good, if we only make the knot harder, we should leave it to the angels of God, and save the wheat grown in our tangled lives.[6]

Notes *

1. J. L. Moreno, *Sociometry, Experimental Method and the Science of Society*, (Beacon, N. Y.: Beacon House, Inc., 1951), p. 108.

2. J. L. Moreno, *The Theatre of Spontaneity*, (New York: Beacon House, Inc., 1947), p. 91.

3. "News and Notes," *The American Journal of Psychiatry*, Volume 104, (May, 1948), p. 748.

4. Cecile Starr, "Films and Mental Health," *Pastoral Psychology*, June, 1952, p. 57.

5. Perry E. Gresham, "Disciplines of the High Calling," *The Shane Quarterly*, January, 1953, pp. 15-16. (Permission also of Bethany Press.)

6. Joseph Fort Newton, *Everyday Religion*, (New York: Abingdon-Cokesbury Press, 1950), p. 97.

* With the exception of quotations reprinted from works in the public domain all excerpts are used by special permission of the preesnt copyright holders.

BIBLIOGRAPHY

Books

Ames, Edward Scribner. *The Psychology of Religious Experience*. Boston: Houghton Mifflin Co., 1910.

Ames, Edward Scribner. "My Conception of God," *Contemporary Religious Thought, an Anthology*. Compiled by Thomas S. Kepler. New York: Abingdon-Cokesbury Press, 1941.

Ashton, Joseph N. *Music in Worship*. Boston: The Pilgrim Press, 1943.

Atkinson, Brooks (ed.). *The Complete Essays and other Writings of Ralph Waldo Emerson*. New York: Random House, Inc., 1940.

Black, James. *The Mystery of Preaching*. New York: Fleming H. Revell Co., 1924.

Blackwood, Andrew W. *The Fine Art of Public Worship*. Nashville: Cokesbury Press, 1939.

Bradley, A. C. *Shakespearean Tragedy*. London: Macmillan & Co., Ltd., 1904.

Bushnell, Horace. *Christian Nurture*. New Haven: Yale University Press, 1947.

Buttrick, George A. *Prayer*. New York: Abingdon-Cokesbury Press, 1942.

Buttrick, George A. *Jesus Came Preaching*. New York: Charles Scribner's Sons, 1943.

Chambers, E. K. *Shakespeare: A Survey*. London: Sedgwick & Jackson, Ltd., 1925.

Chaucer. *Canterbury Tales.* An Interlinear Translation by Vincent F. Hopper. Brooklyn, N. Y.: Barron's Educational Series, Inc., 1948.

Cody, Frank W., and Cartmell, Van H. (ed.). *Shakespeare Arranged For Modern Reading.* Garden City, New York: N.D.

Coe, George A. *What Is Christian Education?* New York: Charles Scribner's Sons, 1929.

Dowden, E. *Shakespere in the Literature Primers.* New York: American Book Co., N.D.

Dowden, Edward. *Introduction to Shakespeare.* New York: Charles Scribner's Sons, N.D.

Dreisoerner, Charles. *The Psychology of Liturgical Music.* Kirkwood, Mo.: Maryhurst Press, 1945.

Eastman, Fred, and Wilson, Louis. *Drama in the Church.* New York: Samuel French, Inc., 1942.

Emerson, E. W., and Forbes, W. E. (ed.). *Journals of Ralph Waldo Emerson* 1820-76. Vol. X. Boston: Houghton Mifflin Co., 1914.

Erskine, John. *The Delight of Great Books.* Indianapolis: The Bobbs-Merrill Co., 1928.

Fisk, Margaret Palmer. *The Art of the Rhythmic Choir.* New York: Harper and Brothers, 1950.

Forman, Harry Buxton (ed.). *The Works of Percy Bysshe Shelley.* Vol. III., London: Reeves & Turner, 1880.

Gervinus, G. G. *Shakespeare Commentaries.* London: Smith, Elder & Co., 1892.

Gladden, Washington. *The Christian Pastor and the Working Church.* New York: Charles Scribner's Sons, 1909.

Hartshorne, Hugh. *Character in Human Relations.* New York: Charles Scribner's Sons, 1932.

Hill, Caroline Miles (ed.). *The World's Great Religious Poetry*. New York: Macmillan Co., 1942.

Hiltner, Seward. *Pastoral Counseling*. New York: Abingdon Cokesbury Press, 1949.

Holy Bible. K.J.V.

Homer. *The Iliad*. Translated by Smith, W. B., and Miller, W. New York: The Macmillan Co., 1945.

Hugo, Victor. *Notre Dame De Paris*. New York: H. M. Caldwell & Co., "N.D."

Kennedy, Charles Rann. *The Terrible Meek*. New York: Samuel French, 1912.

Kierkegaard, Søren Aabye. *The Concept of Dread*. Translated by Walter Lowrie. Princeton: University Press, 1946.

Kittredge, George Lyman (ed.). *The Complete Works of Shakespeare*. Boston: Ginn & Company, 1936.

Klein, M., and Rivière, J. *Love, Hate and Reparation*. London: Hogarth Press, Ltd., 1937.

Mencken, H. L. (ed.). *A New Dictionary of Quotations*. New York: Alfred A. Knopf: 1943.

Menninger, Karl A. *Man Against Himself*. New York: Harcourt, Brace and Co., 1938.

Miller, Perry. *Jonathan Edwards*. New York: William Sloane Associates, 1949.

Moreno, J. L. *The Theatre of Spontaneity*. New York: Beacon House, Inc., 1947.

Moreno, J. L. *Sociometry, Experimental Method and The Science of Society*. Beacon, N. Y.: Beacon House, Inc., 1951.

Morley, Christopher (ed.). *John Bartlett's Familiar Quotations*. Boston: Little, Brown & Co., 1948.

Moulton, R. G. *Shakespeare as a Dramatic Artist*. Oxford: At the Clarendon Press, 1906. (Copyright; Oxford University Press, New York)

Moulton, Richard G. *A Short Introduction to the Literature of the Bible*. Boston: D. C. Heath and Company, 1909.

Newton, Joseph Fort. *Everyday Religion*. New York: Abingdon Cokesbury Press, 1950.

Page, Kirby. *Living Prayerfully*. New York: Farrar & Rinehart, Inc., 1941.

Palmer, G. H. *Intimations of Immortality in the Sonnets of Shakespeare*. Boston: Houghton Mifflin Company, 1912.

Parker, Everett C., Inman, Elinor, and Snyder, Ross. *Religious Radio: What to Do and How*. New York: Harper & Brothers, 1948.

Robinson, William. *The Biblical Doctrine of the Church*. St. Louis: The Bethany Press, 1948.

Rogers, Carl R. *Client-Centered Therapy*. Boston: Houghton Mifflin Co., 1951.

Stevenson, Burton (ed.). *The Handbook of Quotations*. Philadelphia: The Blakiston Co., 1944.

Stewart, J. I. M. *Character and Motive in Shakespeare*. New York: Longmans, Green and Co., 1949.

Strong, Augustus Hopkins. *The Great Poets and Their Theology*. Philadelphia: American Baptist Publication Society, 1897.

The Holy Bible. *A.R.S.* New York: Thomas Nelson & Sons. 1901.

The New Testament. R.S.V. New York: Thomas Nelson & Sons. 1946.

Van Doren, Mark. *Shakespeare*. New York: Henry Holt & Co., 1939.

Webster's Twentieth Century Dictionary. Cleveland, Ohio: The World Publishing Company.

Weigle, Luther Allan. *Jesus and The Educational Method.* New York: The Abingdon Press, 1939.

Whale, J. S. *Christian Doctrine.* Cambridge at the University Press: The Syndics of the Cambridge University Press, 1950.

Articles

Altshuler, Ira M. "Four Years' Experience With Music as a Therapeutic Agent at Eloise Hospital," *American Journal of Psychiatry.* Vol. 100. May, 1944. pp. 792-3-4.

Chekhov, Michael. "An Actor Must Have Three Selves," *Theatre Arts,* December, 1952, p. 32.

Dicks, Russell L. "Devotional Literature in Pastoral Care," *Pastoral Psychology,* February, 1950, p. 47.

Encyclopaedia Britannica. 1952. Vol. VII. Article, "Drama."

Gresham, Perry E. "Disciplines of the High Calling," *The Shane Quarterly,* January, 1953, pp. 15—16.

Haas, Alfred B. "The Therapeutic Value of Hymns," *Pastoral Psychology,* December, 1950, p. 39.

Haas, Alfred B. "Hymn Tunes and Emotions," *Pastoral Psychology,* December, 1951, pp. 27-28.

Hatfield, Louis Duane. "Significance of Baptism," *The Christian Evangelist,* October 17, 1945, pp. 1006-7.

Hayes, Helen. "Theatre for the World," *Theatre Arts,* March, 1952, p. 31.

Hewes, Henry. "The Drama Prospers in Pittsburgh," *Theatre Arts,* October, 1952. p. 33.

Jackson, Edgar N. "The Therapeutic Function in Preaching," *Pastoral Psychology*, June, 1950, p. 36.

Johnson, Paul E. "Jesus As Psychologist," *Pastoral Psychology*, December, 1951, p. 18.

Kew, Clifton E., and Kew, Clinton, J. "Group Psychotherapy In a Church Setting," *Pastoral Psychology*, January, 1951, p. 31.

Kramm, Joseph. "Basic Equipment," *New York Times*, July 20, 1952, Sec. 2, p.x.

Menninger, Karl A. "Religious Applications of Psychiatry," *Pastoral Psychology*, April, 1950, p. 15.

"News and Notes" Dept., *The American Journal of Psychiatry*. Vol. 104 (May, 1948), p. 748.

Oates, Wayne E. "The Diagnostic Use of the Bible," *Pastoral Psychology*, December, 1950, p. 46.

Smith, Eugene L. "The Lord's Prayer in Pre-Marital Counseling," *Pastoral Psychology*, October, 1950, p. 34.

Starr, Cecile. "Films and Mental Health," *Pastoral Psychology*, June, 1952, p. 57.

"Theatre Off-Broadway" Dept., "What *Murder in the Cathedral* Did to Garden City," *Theatre Arts*, April, 1952, pp. 94-5.

"Theatre Off-Broadway" Dept. "Pastor Leads Footlighters," *Theatre Arts*, November, 1952, p. 84.

Woodward, Luther E. "Contributions of the Minister to Mental Hygiene," *Pastoral Psychology*, May, 1950, p. 45.

Letter addressed to P. C. Somerville, Ph.D., Sec. American Passion Play, Bloomington, Illinois, dated November 5, 1952, from the writer.

Letter received from P. C. Somerville, Ph.D., Sec. American Passion Play Bloomington, Illinois, dated November 13, 1952, addressed to the writer.

Letter from the Reverend Irvin E. Lunger, Pastor of the University Church of Disciples of Christ, Chicago, Illinois, August 8, 1952.

> The world's a theatre,
> the earth a stage,
> Which God and Nature do
> with actors fill.
> —THOMAS HEYWOOD

That there is drama in life and drama in religion is a fact which none of us will deny, but not many have fully considered the value of the *conscious* use of the dramatic in helping people to achieve maturity. The link the drama can provide between the life of the church and the secular life, the opportunity it provides for dealing constructively with such ideas as guilt and redemption, is inspiringly presented in this study.

It is known that drama has a therapeutic effect, both on audience and performer. In these pages, Louis Duane Hatfield traces the history of therapeutic drama from the earliest examples in the rituals of primitive peoples, through the great period of Greek drama, into the time of miracle and morality plays offered by the church, and on to the present day, when we find the direct use of drama as therapy in psychodrama.

As the author points out, this ben ficial effect can be found in many di ferent types of plays. He examin Shakespeare's work in some deta and finds that religion, in the tru sense of the word, is reflected consi ently. He next considers the the peutic value of worship, analyzin the role of the preacher, the impo of the sacraments, the nature prayer, the healing power of mus and the therapy of counseling.

Having introduced us to the e ments of drama, religion, and theraj Mr. Hatfield skillfully ties all thr together in his explanation of t therapeutics of religious drama, hig lighting his conclusion with speci present-day examples of religio plays and programs using a co sciously therapeutic approach.

As the Twig Is Bent is a stimul ing, valid study, the product of sch arly and finely selective researc Here is a clear modern-day presen tion of the therapeutic values inh ent in drama and the dramatic in t church . . . as a creative force in me ing human needs.